Sunbonnet
FAMILY REUNION
126 WINNING DESIGNS WITH COMPLETE INSTRUCTIONS

Album 1

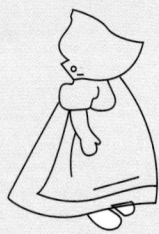

Copyright © 1989 House of White Birches
306 East Parr Road, Berne, Indiana 46711

ALL RIGHTS RESERVED. No part of this book may be reproduced in any form or by any means without the prior written permission of the Publisher, excepting brief quotes in connection with reviews written specifically for inclusion in a magazine or newspaper.

Library of Congress Catalog Number: 89-81185
ISBN: 1-882138-01-5

Sunbonnet Family Reunion, Album I

Editor: Sandra Hatch
Art Director/Writer: Ken Tate
Artist: Vicki Macy
Photography: Rhonda Davis, Nancy Sharp, Mary Joynt, Brent Long
Production: Sandra Ridgway

House of White Birches

Publishers: Carl H. Muselman
Arthur K. Muselman
Chief Executive Officer: John Robinson
Marketing Director: Scott Moss

Every effort has been made to have patterns and instructions in *Sunbonnet Family Album* as accurate as possible. Most of these patterns are original designs. We have attempted to accurately credit those few that are adaptations of previously published patterns. However, we cannot be responsible for problems you might encounter in constructing these pieces, human errors or typographical mistakes.

INTRODUCTION

Sunbonnet Sue and her friends have fascinated quilters for generations. Bertha Corbett and the other artists credited with creating Sunbonnet drawings could not have known how quilters would adopt this faceless child and treat her like one of their own.

While working on a Sunbonnet publication in the past, I fell in love with Sunbonnet Sue all over again. I had forgotten the many hours of enjoyment I had spent with my husband making a Sunbonnet quilt almost 20 years ago.

It all began because we wanted to make a quilt together. We found a pattern for a simple Sunbonnet Sue and decided that it looked easy enough for a beginning project. Finding the fabrics wasn't difficult since I had always been a seamstress and had made crazy scrap quilts as a child. I remember sorting through fabrics, trying to color-coordinate Sue's dresses and hats. My husband helped with the sewing which was done with a zigzag stitch using black thread on the sewing machine. We made 40 blocks. When the blocks were complete, they were set aside and were not stitched together into a top for several years. It was finally tied and put to use.

That quilt is still being used on our bed at our camp. Just this summer I brought it home to repair some of the frayed edges. While working on it, I remembered the hours we spent together sewing. It seems like a lifetime ago! I am so glad Sue remembers it all so that she can keep reminding me as time goes by!

I know that you will find a pattern in this book that will provide you with many fun-filled hours, and once you begin you won't be able to stop. The contest that precipitated this book (and the three books to follow) had 504 entries, and 126 of them are found in this book. Every block, winner and non-winner alike, will be shared to inspire you to be creative and get started on a quilt right away.

Before you begin to think about sewing, take the time to look through this whole book. Study each Sunbonnet pattern and notice the details. Get to know this sweet little character and, before you know it, you'll fall in love with her just like the rest of us; and who knows how many wonderful quilts will result!

Sunbonnet

	PAGE		PAGE
Introduction	2	Family 11 Patterns	123
Bertha L. Corbett	4	Family 12 Patterns	132
Dorothymae and Harold Groves	5	Family 13 Patterns	142
Family 1	7	Family 14 Patterns	151
Family 2	8	Index	160
Family 3	9		
Family 4	10		
Family 5	11		
Family 6	12		
Family 7	13		
Family 8	14		
Family 9	15		
Family 10	16		
Family 11	17		
Family 12	18		
Family 13	19		
Family 14	20		
General Instructions	21		
Family 1 Patterns	25		
Family 2 Patterns	35		
Family 3 Patterns	47		
Family 4 Patterns	56		
Family 5 Patterns	66		
Family 6 patterns	75		
Family 7 Patterns	86		
Family 8 Patterns	96		
Family 9 Patterns	105		
Family 10 Patterns	114		

About Our Cover

Our cover quilt piece, "Sue Makes a Quilt," was designed and appliqued by Linda M. Throckmorton of Cutler, Maine. Linda's design earned her a ribbon and prize in the first Sunbonnet Family Reunion, sponsored by Groves Publishing Company of Kansas City. She was one of 41 prize winners in the contest. Linda's pattern may be found on page 33 of this edition.

FAMILY REUNION
126 WINNING DESIGNS WITH COMPLETE INSTRUCTIONS

Bertha L. Corbett
Mother of the Sunbonnet Babies

Quilters have long known that quilting is a form of art.

What quilter hasn't felt the onrush of creative spirit as she sat down to her work? It then seems only natural that an artist would contribute much to the art of quiltmaking.

Such is the story of Bertha L. Corbett Melcher, the "Mother of the Sunbonnet Babies."

Bertha Corbett began her career in Minneapolis, Minn., and later spent a year of training with illustrator Howard Pyle. It was during her time in Minneapolis, around the turn of the century, that Bertha conceived the idea of her Babies and proved they were not just another pretty face.

In fact, they had no faces at all.

During a social gathering of several artist friends, one observed that a faceless figure displays little emotional expression. Bertha remembered seeing a small girl, her face hidden by a large sunbonnet. The child's faceless beauty caused her to remark, "I don't think a face is necessary in order to make a figure expressive." Challenged to prove her point by the other artists, Bertha picked up her pen and drew her first Sunbonnet Baby.

Bertha's work so captivated the artists and, later, a growing group of admirers, that she began to devote more and more of her time to her nursery of characters. First a book and then a children's primer were produced to satisfy people's hunger for more and more of the Babies.

Later, Bertha—who also wrote much of the verse accompanying the illustrations—turned the concept into a popular comic strip.

She also became a popular guest on the lecture and vaudeville circuit.

On one visit to Los Angeles, Bertha spoke at social and professional functions and delivered several lectures on her creation. At all these functions she sported what one newspaper called her "quaint conceit… a stick pin mounted with a tiny medallion showing her trademark—a bewitching little sunbonnet baby a quarter of an inch long."

Bertha was described as "a slender, brown-haired girl with a face filled with animation, expressive eyes and a smile at once frank and winning. She loves children or she could never draw them so sympathetically and charmingly as she does, so that every woman who looks at one wants to take it up in her arms and cuddle it."

The Babies seemed to take on a life of their own. They became the subject of holiday greeting cards. They adorned advertising and promotional material, including the popular—and still marketed—Dutch Cleanser®. Bertha often joked that she expected a visit from the Labor Commission because, "the Babies are so very young to be made to earn a living for me."

Bertha made two moral stipulations for the use of her Babies in the earning of her living: "One was that my Sunbonnet Babies shall never be guilty of being saucy to their elders, and the other was that they should never under any circumstances be spanked!"

Soon "Overall Boys" began to accompany the Sunbonnet Girls to all important functions. Together, the pair, in all their various sizes and shapes, were shown in almost every conceivable childhood activity and chore.

The revival of interest in Bertha Corbett's work came about through the labors of some of the country's best quilt designers. The faceless children have a timeless quality about them, the perfect qualification for quilting. So, in addition to all of the Sunbonnet memorabilia being collected and printed, there is also a continual interest in the Babies as quilting models.

It is fitting that the work of Bertha Corbett be recognized in the quilting world. Through her art at the turn of the last century, the art of quilting has been elevated to new heights as we near the turn of this century.

By Ken Tate

Dorothymae and Harold Groves
Sunbonnet Entrepreneurs

Sunbonnet Girls and Overall Boys are a way of life for Dorothymae and Harold Groves of Kansas City.

The Groves, who conceived, compiled and now are touring the Sunbonnet Family

Reunion contest, have become Sunbonnet entrepreneurs in their own right. In addition to the contest, Harold and Dorothymae operate Groves Publishing Company, specializing in Sunbonnet memorabilia.

Their wares include 11 reprinted books of Bertha L. Corbett Melcher, Sunbonnet greeting cards, plus dozens of pieces of Sunbonnet gift items. Additionally, Harold compiled the *Kansas City Star's* classic quilt patterns in 10 volumes.

Dorothymae's love of Sunbonnet Babies began with Sunbonnet tole paintings in 1968, painted for the couple's three daughters. In 1982, she quilted her first Sunbonnet Baby quilt from a top pieced by her late mother-in-law.

In 1988, the couple began collecting

Continued on next page

postcards, ink blotters, calendars, books and dishes of Sunbonnets. They now have over 330 postcards dated from 1903 to the 1920s, with many in complete series.

The high point of Dorothymae's involvement with sunbonnets came in July 1989, when she spent three days with Ruth Melcher Thom, the second daughter of Bertha Corbett Melcher.

The Groves compiled 504 Sunbonnet quilt designs for the *Sunbonnet Family Reunion*. The blocks came from entrants from 6 to 83 years of age. In addition to entries from the United States and Canada, the Groves received blocks from the Netherlands and Australia.

Dorothymae says her love of Sunbonnets stems from the fact that, because the Babies' faces never show, there is no connection of racial, ethnic or national characteristics to them, making them "international quilt figures."

She also says the quilts and their models "make you smile without seeing a smile."

Dorothymae is a recognized quilter in her own right. In addition to many "best of show" ribbons at state fairs, she has also seen one of her quilts displayed at Disneyland.

Dorothymae says she could never have completed the work on the Sunbonnet Family Reunion contest without the help of Harold, who not only built the display panels, but also ironed each of the blocks for mounting for the tour and exhibit.

Harold travels with Dorothymae to virtually all the show she attends. The Groves have taken the Reunion exhibit to over a dozen sites, with several more planned.

They are also planning the next Reunion contest, scheduled for the summer and fall of 1990.

Sunbonnet FAMILY 1
FAMILY REUNION

See Page 25	See Page 26	See Page 28
See Page 29	See Page 30	See Page 31
See Page 32	See Page 33	See Page 34

"I don't think a face is necessary in order to make a figure expressive."

—Bertha L. Corbett

Poetry excerpts from *The Sunbonnet Babies*, *What's on the Air?*, and *The Sunbonnet Babies at Work, at Play* by Bertha Corbett, reprinted by Groves Publishing Company, Kansas City, Mo.

Sunbonnet Family Reunion

See Page 35	See Page 36	See Page 38
See Page 39	See Page 40	See Page 42
See Page 43	See Page 44	See Page 45

Sunbonnet FAMILY 2
FAMILY REUNION

See the little chicks we feed;
Such a lot of care they need.
Little chicks don't make a fuss;
But turkey gobblers frighten us.

Sunbonnet FAMILY REUNION — FAMILY 3

See Page 47	See Page 48	See Page 49
See Page 50	See Page 51	See Page 52
See Page 53	See Page 54	See Page 55

To "trip the light fantastic toe"
We tune in on the Radio,
And with the music we adore
We "make believe" a ball-room floor.

Sunbonnet Family Reunion 9

See Page 56	See Page 57	See Page 59
See Page 60	See Page 61	See Page 62
See Page 63	See Page 64	See Page 65

Sunbonnet FAMILY REUNION — FAMILY 4

With bent pins we wait for fish
But no bites answer our wish.

Sunbonnet FAMILY REUNION — FAMILY 5

See Page 66	See Page 67	See Page 68
See Page 69	See Page 70	See Page 71
See Page 72	See Page 73	See Page 74

So with all our thoughts joy-turning
We keep our Christmas Candles burning
And by magic Radio
Send gleams to all we know.

Sunbonnet Family Reunion

See Page 75	See Page 76	See Page 77
See Page 78	See Page 79	See Page 81
See Page 83	See Page 84	See Page 85

Sunbonnet FAMILY 6
FAMILY REUNION

Bookworms spin silken threads of thought.
Finest fancies ever wrought
In a cocoon called a Book
Wherein young or old may look.

Sunbonnet FAMILY REUNION FAMILY 7

Now when the morning comes
They wake and start at once to mend,
For on their needle handiwork
Their dollies must depend.

See Page 86	See Page 87	See Page 88
See Page 89	See Page 90	See Page 91
See Page 92	See Page 94	See Page 95

Sunbonnet Family Reunion 13

See Page 96	See Page 97	See Page 98
See Page 99	See Page 100	See Page 101
See Page 102	See Page 103	See Page 104

Sunbonnet FAMILY REUNION — Family 8

Here we come! Here we come!
Bringing a red Geranium!

Sunbonnet FAMILY REUNION FAMILY 9

See Page 105	See Page 106	See Page 107
See Page 108	See Page 109	See Page 110
See Page 111	See Page 112	See Page 113

In our memory garden of Radio
Friendship's sweetest flowers grow
In a sheltered corner, near the gate
Jack's Mother's Johnny-jump-ups wait.

Sunbonnet Family Reunion 15

See Page 114	See Page 115	See Page 116
See Page 117	See Page 118	See Page 119
See Page 120	See Page 121	See Page 122

Sunbonnet FAMILY REUNION FAMILY 10

Happy hearts from loving deeds
Grow, as flowers do, from seeds.
Plant the seeds of Joy, my dears,
Water well, and weed out fears.

Sunbonnet FAMILY REUNION FAMILY 11

See Page 123	See Page 124	See Page 125
See Page 126	See Page 127	See Page 128
See Page 129	See Page 130	See Page 131

Sometimes we dress up in the style
And play at "Lady" for awhile.

Sunbonnet Family Reunion   17

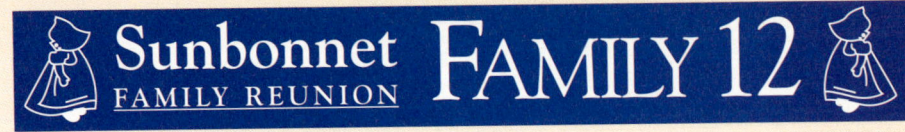

See Page 132	See Page 133	See Page 134
See Page 135	See Page 136	See Page 138
See Page 139	See Page 140	See Page 141

Sunbonnet FAMILY REUNION FAMILY 12

Such love can lead but to one end,
'Tis nature's own disposal.
That "yum-yum-yum" behind the wall
Brought forth a sweet proposal.

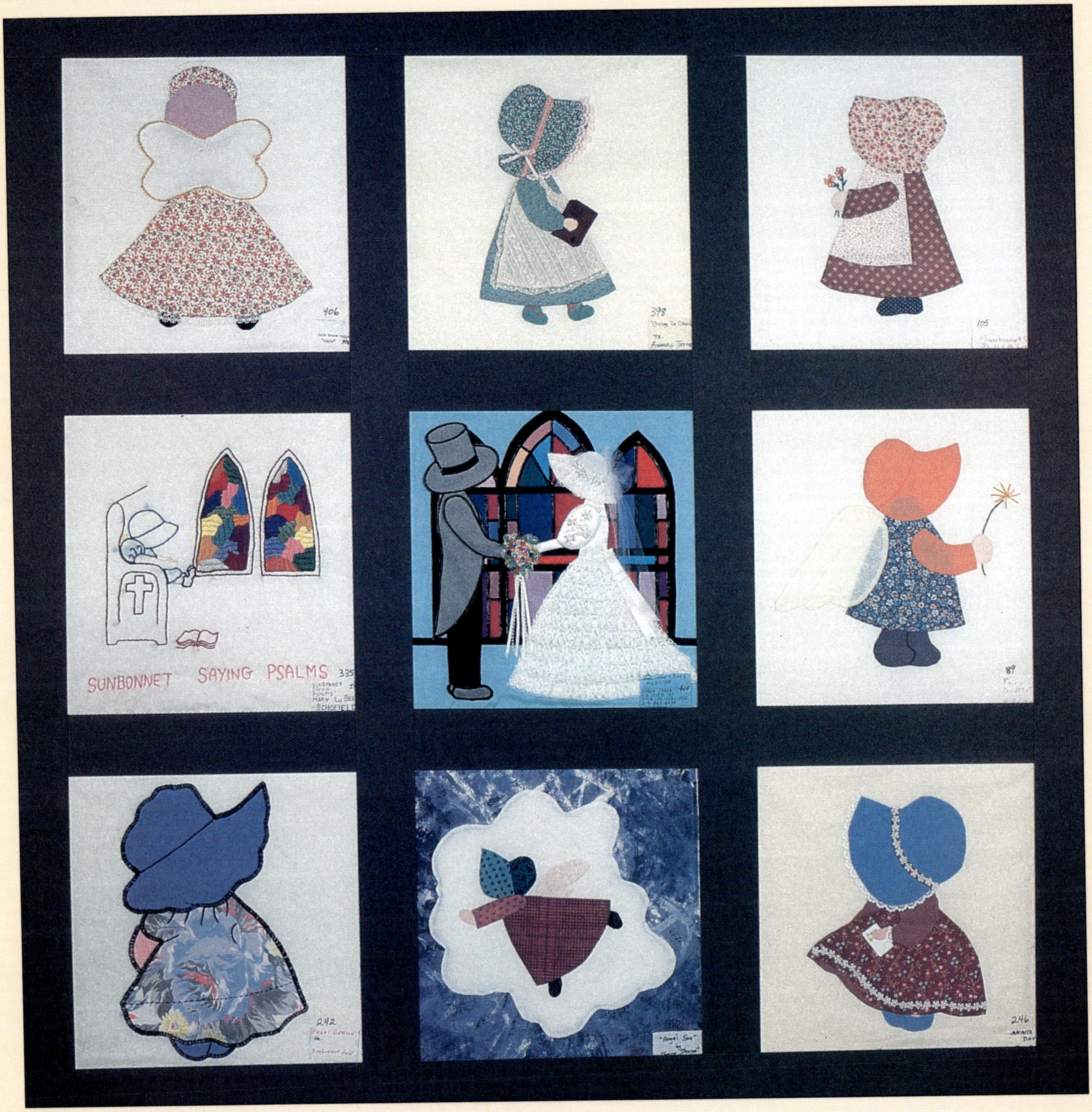

Sunbonnet Family Reunion — FAMILY 13

See Page 142	See Page 143	See Page 144
See Page 145	See Page 146	See Page 147
See Page 148	See Page 149	See Page 150

Of course we've many calls to pay
So we go out each pleasant day.

Sunbonnet FAMILY 14
FAMILY REUNION

See Page 151	See Page 152	See Page 153
See Page 154	See Page 155	See Page 156
See Page 157	See Page 158	See Page 159

"Sunbonnet Babies shall never be guilt of being saucy to their elders, and they shall never, under any circumstances, be spanked."
—Bertha Corbett

20 Sunbonnet Family Reunion

Sunbonnet
FAMILY REUNION
General Instructions

All but one of the blocks shown in this book are appliqued designs. Each block was designed to fit a 12" background square. If you want a larger block, you may enlarge the pattern as desired.

Applique is the process of applying one piece of fabric on top of another for decorative or functional purposes. The functional purpose is generally in the form of a patch to cover a damaged portion of a garment or other fabric covering. Decorative applique can be part of clothing, quilts, pillows, furniture and most any other fabric item that might need a bit of design or color to brighten it.

Applique is popular because one can almost paint pictures with the fabric pieces. Flowers, animals, architecture and even human faces can be portrayed in fabric through the process of applique. Piecing can result in some of the same designs, but the look is not the same. Applique is rich and flowing.

Before the actual applique begins, the background block needs to be cut (at least 1/2" larger all around than desired finished size) and prepared for stitching. Most applique designs are centered on the block in some manner. To find the center of your background square, fold in half, and in half again, and crease with your fingers. Now unfold and fold diagonally and crease again. Repeat for other corners.

You now have a block with center-line creases to help you position your design. Some people just like to place their pieces as they wish, but others like to be very precise. If you have a full-size drawing of your design, as is given with the Sunbonnets in this book, you might like to draw the design on your background block to help with placement. This is most easily accomplished by first transferring the design to a large piece of paper. Tracing paper would be the easiest kind to use. Place paper on top of the design and, using masking tape, tape to hold in place. Trace design onto paper.

If you have a light box, the next step would be easy. Many people do not have one of these helpful devices. Inventive quilters have found that a large window works almost as well. Stand up close and tape your pattern on the window while you trace your design onto your background block with a water-erasable marker or chalk pencil. This drawing will show you exactly where your fabric pieces should be placed on your background block.

Once your design has been transferred to your background, you must prepare templates for each shape that requires applique. Templates are made for each piece by tracing off shapes one at a time. You should use something stiff for this step—cardboard or plastic template material made especially for this purpose may be used. Draw the shape of your design onto your template material. If you are accustomed to using templates with seam allowance added, at this time, draw another line around your shape 1/4" away from the first line. For machine applique, a seam allowance is not necessary. Most hand appliquers prefer to leave the seam allowance off the template and add it to the shape during the cutting process. Cut out the template on your drawn line.

There are many techniques one can use to applique. The most traditional is hand applique. The preferred method is to use a template made from the desired finished shape without seam allowance added. Fabrics are chosen (100 percent cotton is recommended) and pre-washed to prevent the bleeding of color to the background block once the block is finished. When prewashing is done and the fabric has been ironed, trace the desired shape onto the right side of the fabric with a water-erasable marker, light lead or white chalk pencil. Leave at least 1/2" between design motifs when tracing to allow for the seam allowance when cutting out your shapes. When the desired number of shapes needed have been drawn on your fabric pieces, cut out shapes leaving 1/8" - 1/4" all around drawn line for turning under. Some applique experts advise you to stitch around the shape just outside the turning line to give you a guide for the turning line. This keeps the piece from stretching out of shape as you work with it. This is an optional step.

Freezer paper applique has been popular in recent years. The purpose of using freezer paper is to help you make your shape conform exactly to the shape of the template used for your design. Cut the finished shape out of freezer paper and iron the shiny side onto the wrong side of fabric. Cut out shape 1/4" larger around paper pattern, clip curves and iron seam allowances under. Remove paper before applique if desired, or leave inside during applique process and remove by pulling through a small opening left at the end before final stitches are taken, or by cutting away background from back and pulling the paper from underneath when block is finished. The English paper-piecing method is done in a similar fashion, except, in many of the older quilts, the paper was never removed when the quilt was completed.

If you do not use paper as a guide for turning your edges under and making smooth shapes, you might want to turn your shape's edges over on the drawn or stitched line (if you machine stitched around your design). When turning the edges under, remember to make sharp corners sharp and smooth edges smooth. Your fabric patch should retain the shape of the template used to cut it.

Basting the edges over may be helpful to some stitchers. When the edges are basted over before the actual applique process, the shape is already formed and it does help to make the process easier. Some stitchers prefer to turn the edge under with their needle as they work rather than take the time necessary for hand basting. Experiment with several methods and choose the one that works best for you or invent one of your own!

Machine applique can be as beautiful as hand applique but in some circumstances this is not easy to accomplish. There are several new products available to help make the process easier and faster.

Some stitchers advocate the use of a product called Wonder Under® by Pellon. This product has paper on one side. To use, dry-iron it onto the wrong side of your fabric. Draw desired shapes onto the paper and cut them out. Peel off paper, position on the right side of your background block and dry-iron in place. Your shape will stay in place until you have machine stitched all around it. This process does add a little bulk or stiffness to the appliqued shape and may make quilting through the layers by hand more difficult.

Another product that helps make applique easier and stabilizes your background fabric is called Stitch-N-Tear®. This is placed under the background fabric while machine applique is being done, and then torn away when work is finished. This kind of stabilizer helps to keep the background fabric from pulling during the machine applique process.

During the actual applique process, you will be layering one shape on top of another. Where two fabrics overlap, the underneath piece does not have to be turned under or stitched down. If possible, the underneath fabric should be trimmed away when block is finished. This is done by carefully cutting away the background from underneath and then cutting away unnecessary layers. Quilting through several layers by hand is not an easy process.

After positioning fabric shapes on your background block, pin or baste them in place. Using a blind or applique stitch, sew pieces in place with matching thread and small stitches. Start with background pieces first and work up to foreground pieces. If you would like to add dimension to your pieces, a bit of stuffing may be inserted in a piece before the final stitches are made. Be sure that the stuffing is distributed evenly before final stitches are made. Do not cut away background fabric from beneath stuffed areas.

The patterns given in this book require some added detail work with embroidery stitches. Many shapes are too small to be appliqued but are integral parts of the design. These shapes are added with embroidery floss. If you refer to the colored photograph of each block, you will be able to see the details. In some cases, they could be eliminated, if you prefer not to add them. However, these little details do add a great deal to the finished looks of the blocks. Diagrams of the most common stitches are given here. Note: Color and stitch recommendations may be changed to suit your own stitching tastes.

Special shapes require special skills. The diagrams shown provide some extra help in successful completion of applique of these shapes. Be sure to refer to this guide, as well as the color photographs at the beginning of this book when working on your blocks.

Appliqué Stitch Guide

Corners: To make a neat square corner, fold in one edge of the piece 1/4" or on seam line to the wrong side; then fold over second edge. For corners that have very pointed edges, such as a leaf, fold down tip first, then fold in sides. Excess fabric might need to be trimmed.

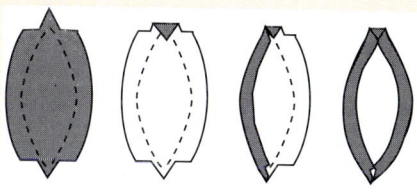

Pointed Corners: Clip off seam allowance to 1/8" below point. Fold point over at tip to seam allowance. Fold in trimmed sides at seam line. This method is most commonly needed when appliquéing leaves.

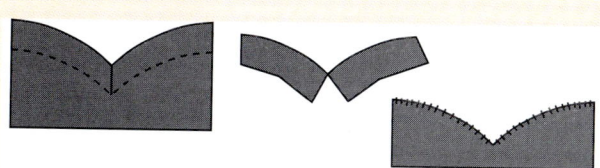

Inside Corners: If a sharp dip is part of the shape, such as in the heart design, clip into the seam allowance to the point. Fold in raw edges to the wrong side. Stitches will need to be done very close together at the indented spot.

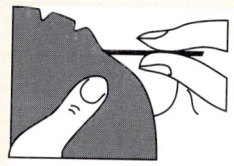

Curved Edges: Difficult curved edges are easy to work with by using the needle to turn the seam allowance under as you stitch.

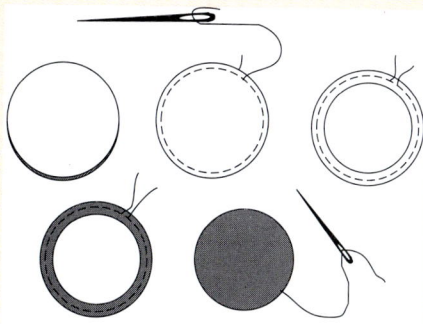

Circles: Cut a cardboard template the size of the finished circle. Sew a basting stitch around fabric piece on seam line. Place fabric piece centered over template and pull basting stitches to gather piece around cardboard shape. Press gently with iron and pull out template. Sew in place.

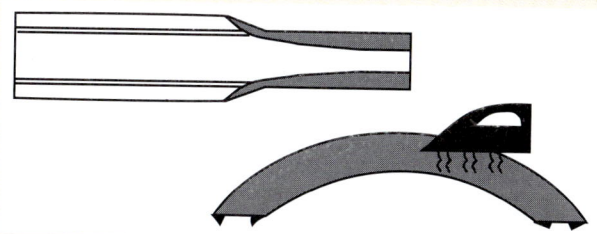

Stems: Stem pieces for flowers and leaves are usually cut on the fabric's bias or diagonal grain. This helps them to curve easily. There are special tools that can help you make your bias strips, or you may purchase premade bias tape. It is not always available in the colors you need. If you have no tools available, you might make a cardboard template in the required finished width; fold the fabric around it and press in place. Press and place on fabric.

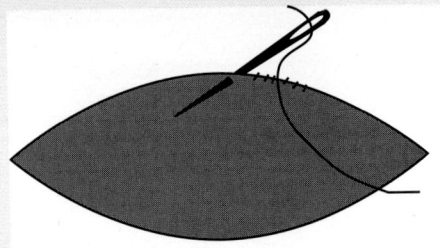

Appliqué Stitch: Use a close slipstitch or blind stitch to secure the pieces to the background.

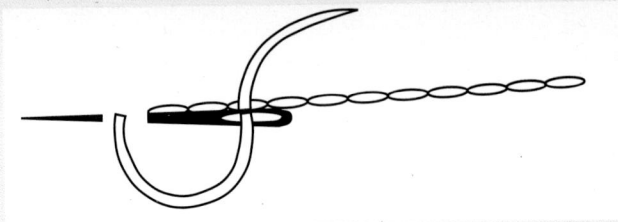

Backstitch: Use for outlining.

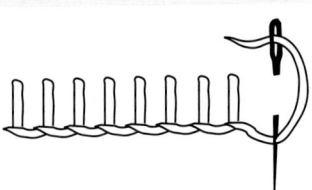

Blanket Stitch: May be used to finish raw edge of appliqué.

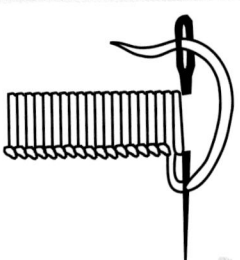

Buttonhole Stitch: Used to finish raw edge to keep from fraying.

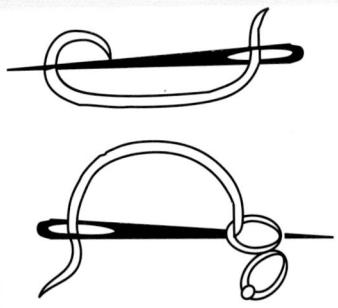

Lazy-Daisy Stitch: Use this stitch to make flower

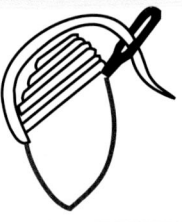

Satin Stitch: A nice stitch to cover small areas. Edges should be neat.

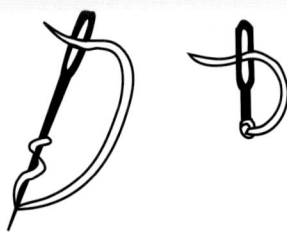

French Knot: Use for flower centers and filling small spaces. It creates a textured effect.

Long & Short Stitch: Use for shading with several colors or to fill in a large space.

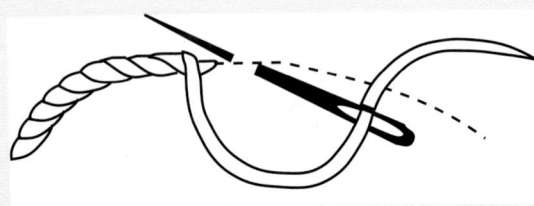

Stem Stitch: Use when a narrow outline is needed.

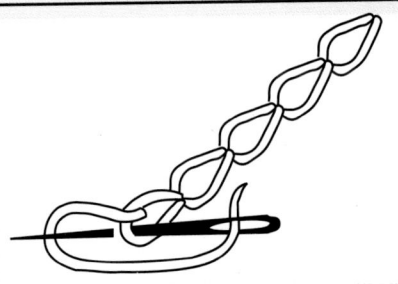

Chain Stitch: Use this stitch to make flower petals.

Betsy Sue Ross/All-American Sue
Marge Eakins • La Puente, CA

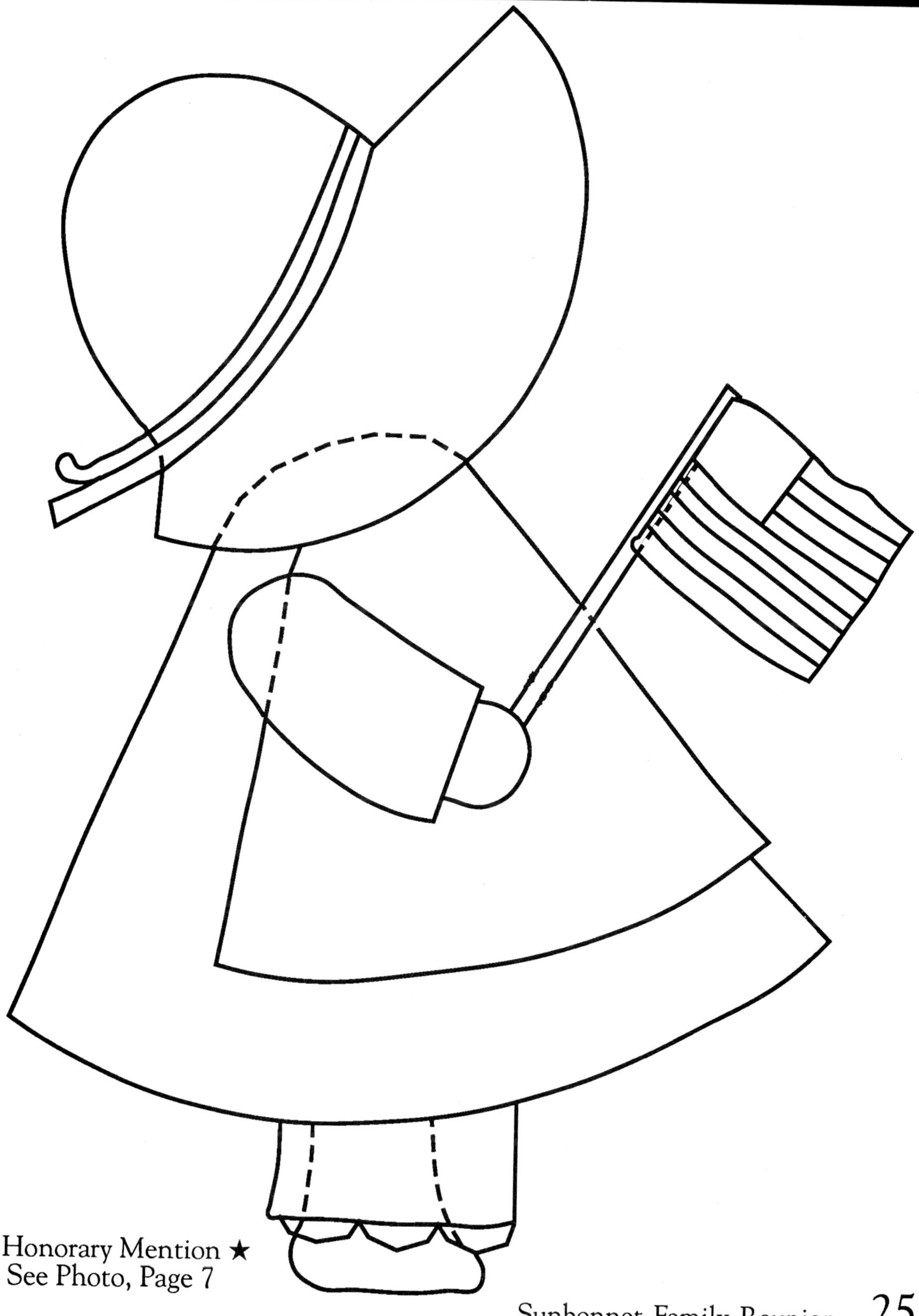

★ Honorary Mention ★
See Photo, Page 7

★ Bertha Corbett Award ★
See Photo, Page 7
Match to Sunbonnet Template,
Previous Page

Sunbonnet Family Reunion 27

Sunbonnet FAMILY REUNION

Checked Sue
Kati Olson • Wyoming, MN

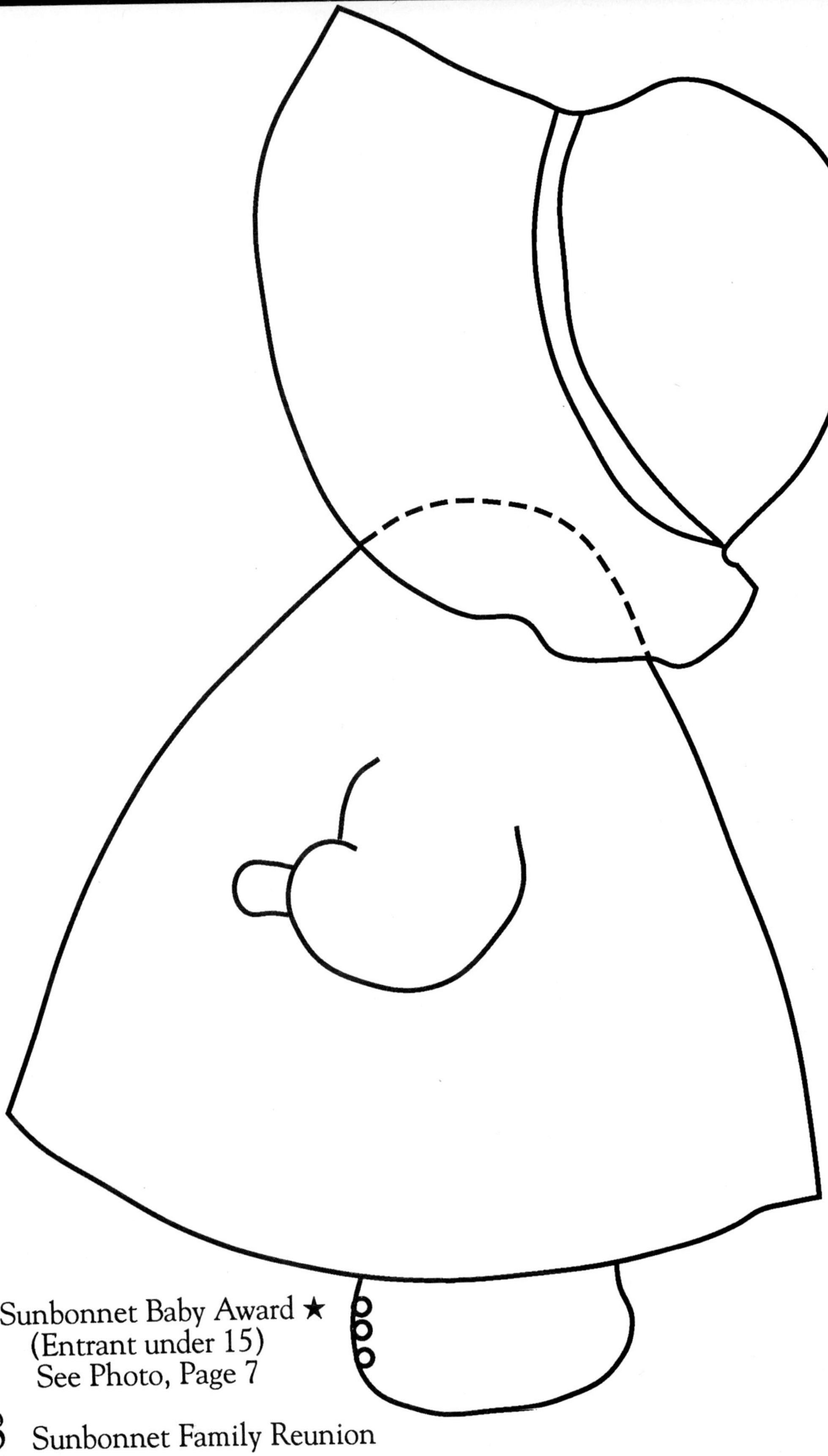

★ Sunbonnet Baby Award ★
(Entrant under 15)
See Photo, Page 7

Old Dutch Girl
Leona E. Price • Florissant, MO

★ Old Dutch Cleanser Award ★
See Photo, Page 7

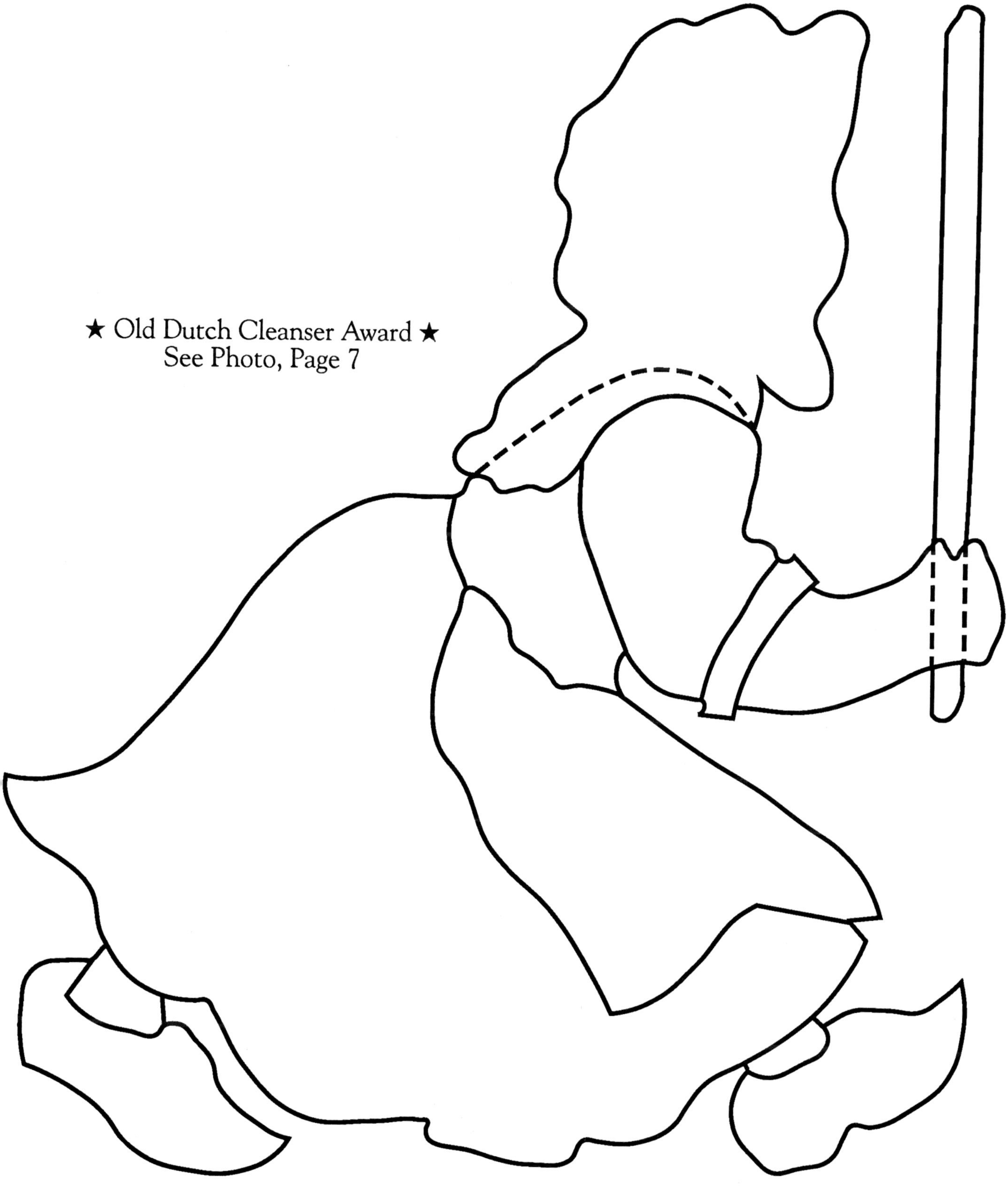

Sunbonnet FAMILY REUNION

Choretime Sue
Mildred Fauquet • Lincoln, NE

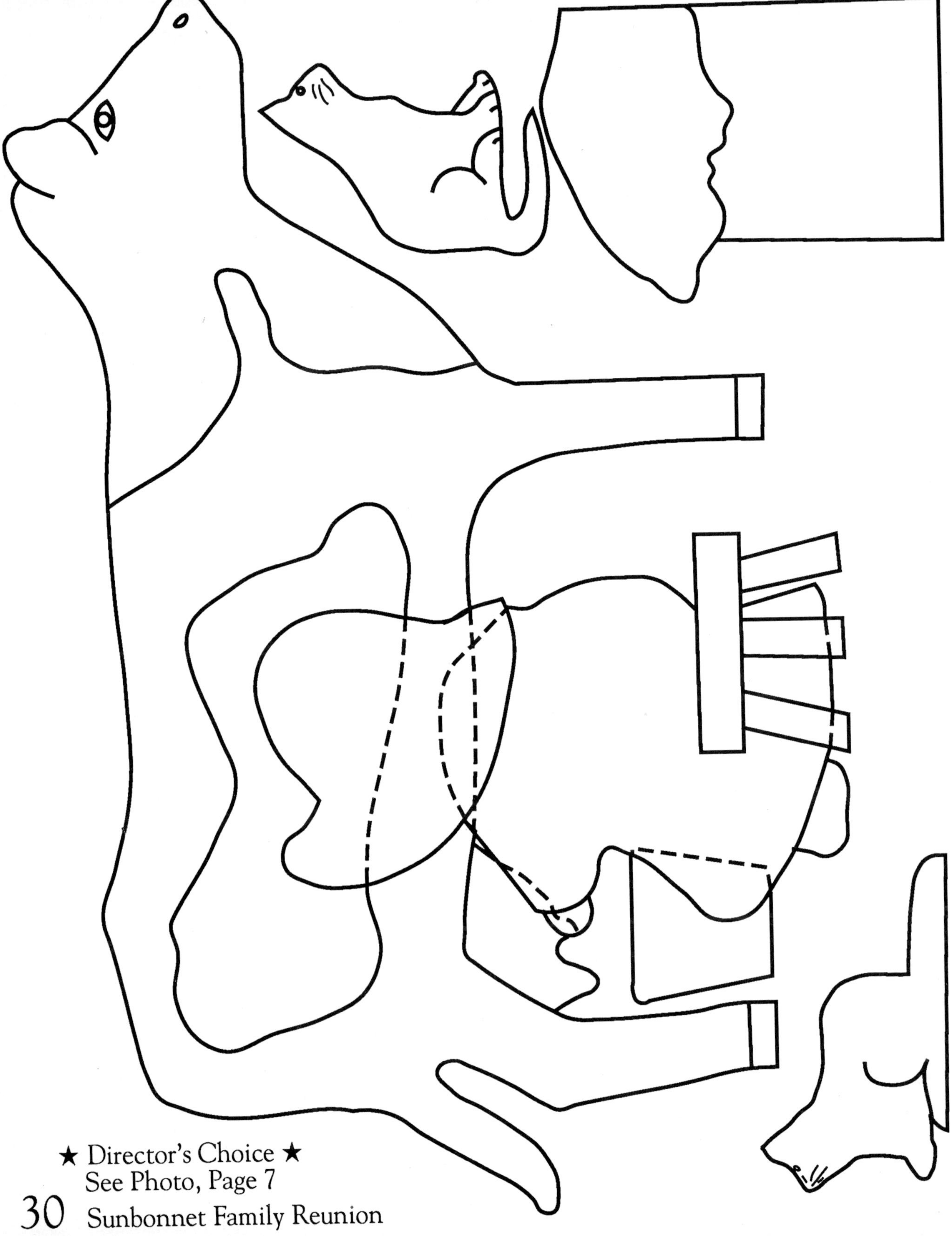

★ Director's Choice ★
See Photo, Page 7

Feeding Chickens
Nurlie Foster • Haynesville, LA

★ Honorary Mention ★
See Photo, Page 7

Sunbonnet  Girl Scout Cookie Time

Sandra A. Anderson • Lincoln, NE

★ Blue Ribbon ★
See Photo, Page 7

Sue Makes A Quilt
Linda M. Throckmorton • Cutler, ME

★ Blue Ribbon ★
See Photo, Page 7

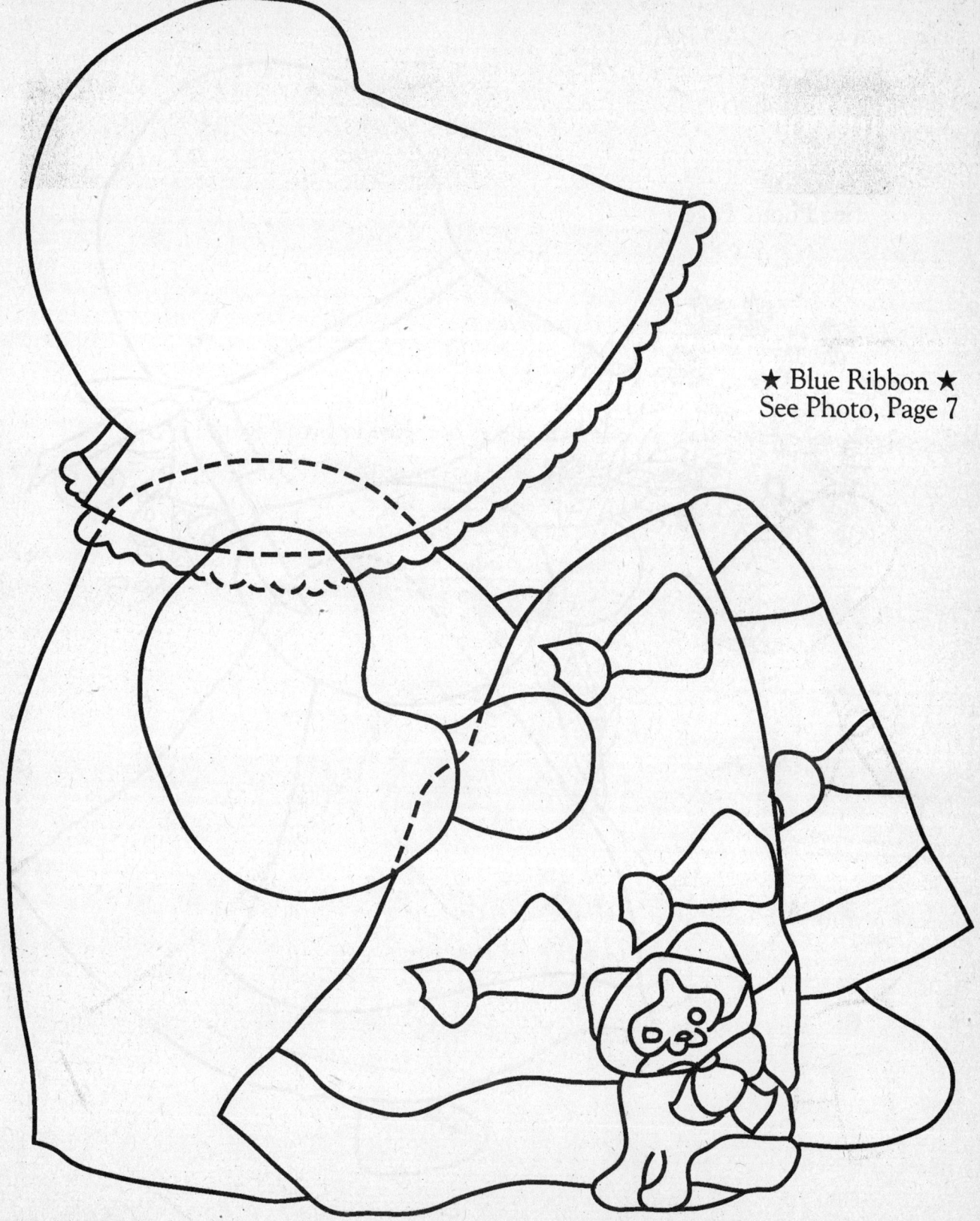

Sunbonnet FAMILY REUNION
Lavender Sue
Evelyn A. Gorek • North Royalton, OH

See Photo, Page 7

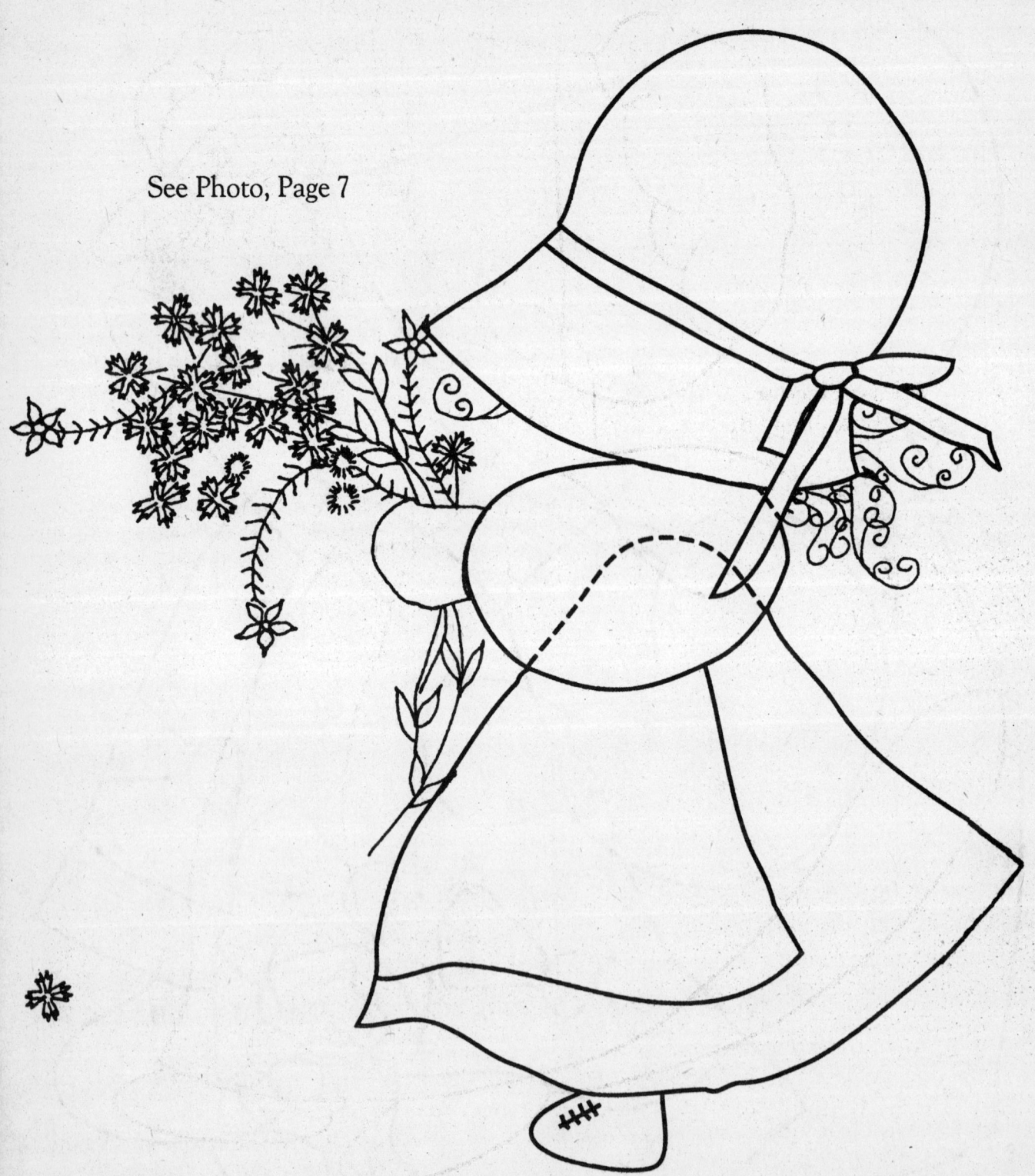

Sunbonnet Girl & Kewpie
Philis R. Alongi • Anaheim, CA

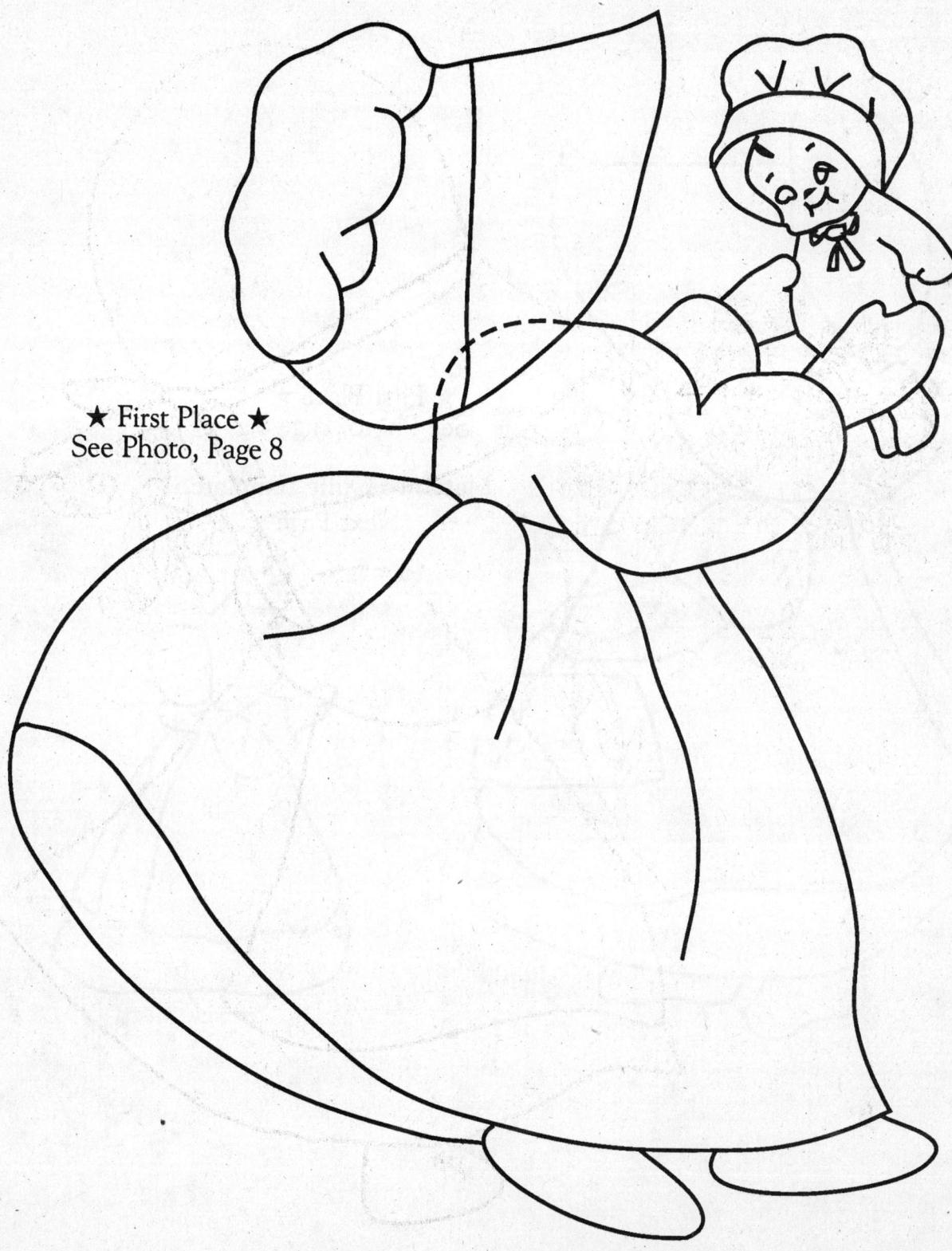

★ First Place ★
See Photo, Page 8

Sunbonnet Family Reunion

Sunbonnet FAMILY REUNION

Look What We Made, Mommy!
Linda Baker • San Clemente, CA

★ First Place ★
See Photo, Page 8

Match to Quilt Template,
Next Page

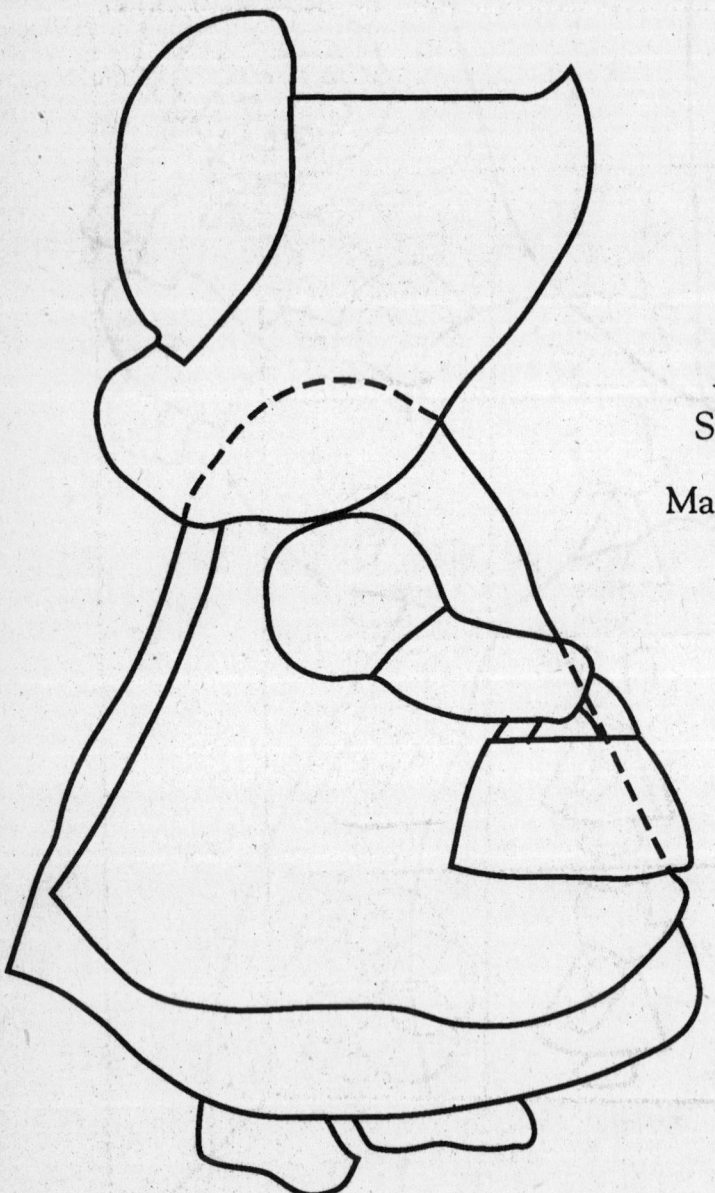

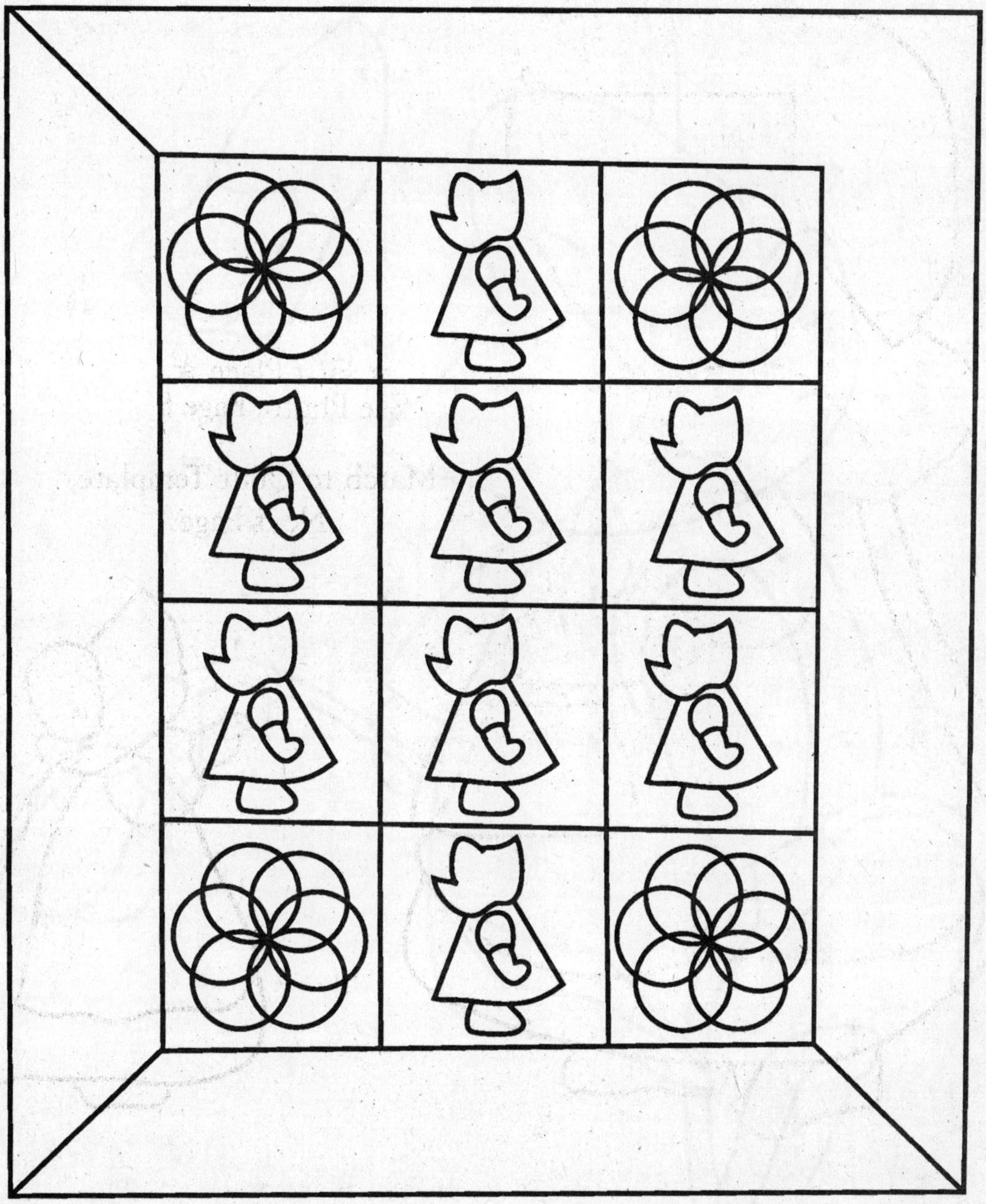

Sunbonnet Family Reunion 37

Sunbonnet FAMILY REUNION

A Botanist's Delight
Eleanor Wright • Santa Barbara, CA

★ First Place ★
See Photo, Page 8

38 Sunbonnet Family Reunion

Bertha Sue
Janelle Jones Knox • Springfield, MO

★ First Place ★
See Photo, Page 8

Sunbonnet FAMILY REUNION

A Mouse!
Ginette Bourque • Kanata, Ont., Canada

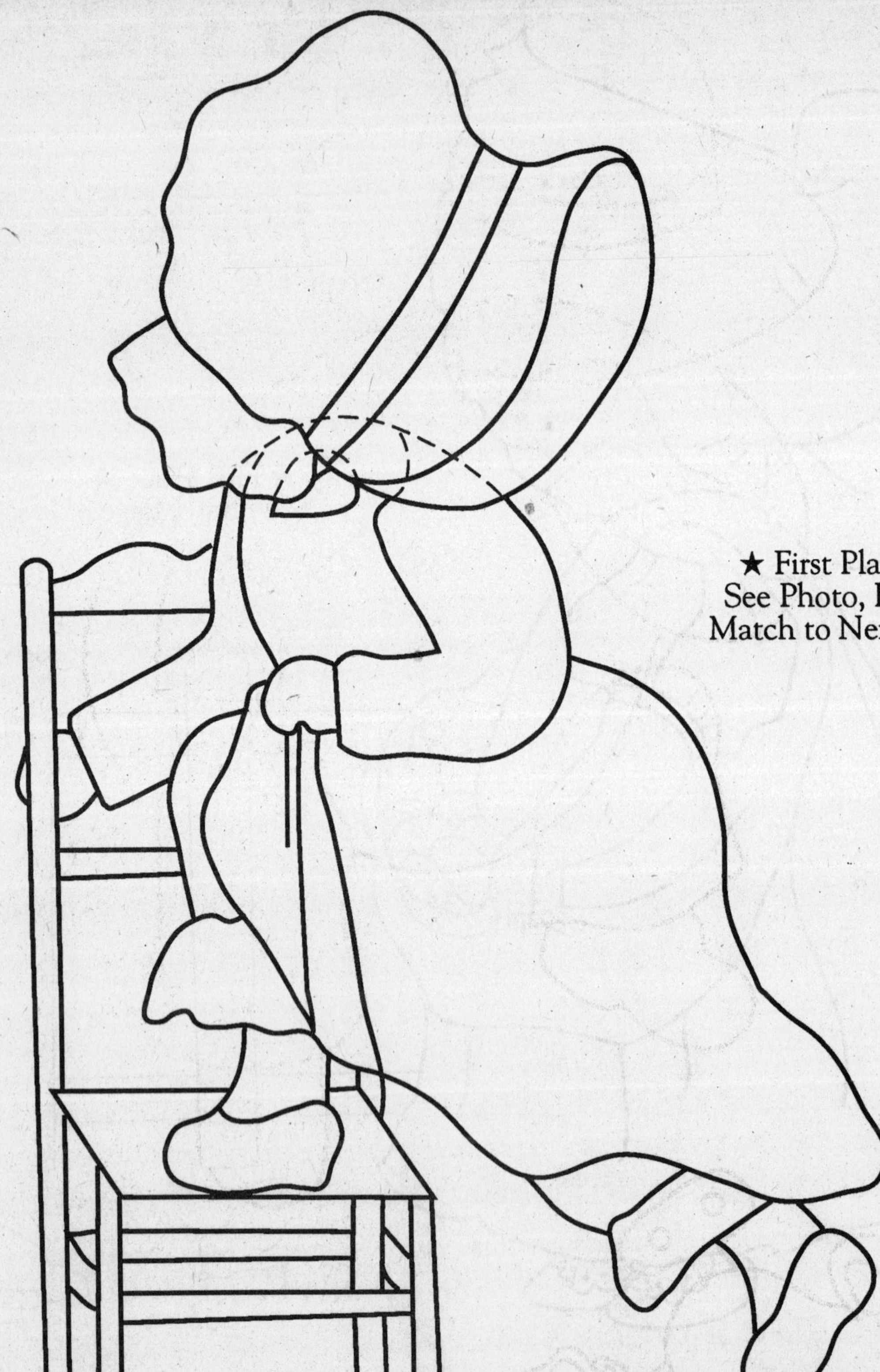

★ First Place ★
See Photo, Page 8
Match to Next Page

40 Sunbonnet Family Reunion

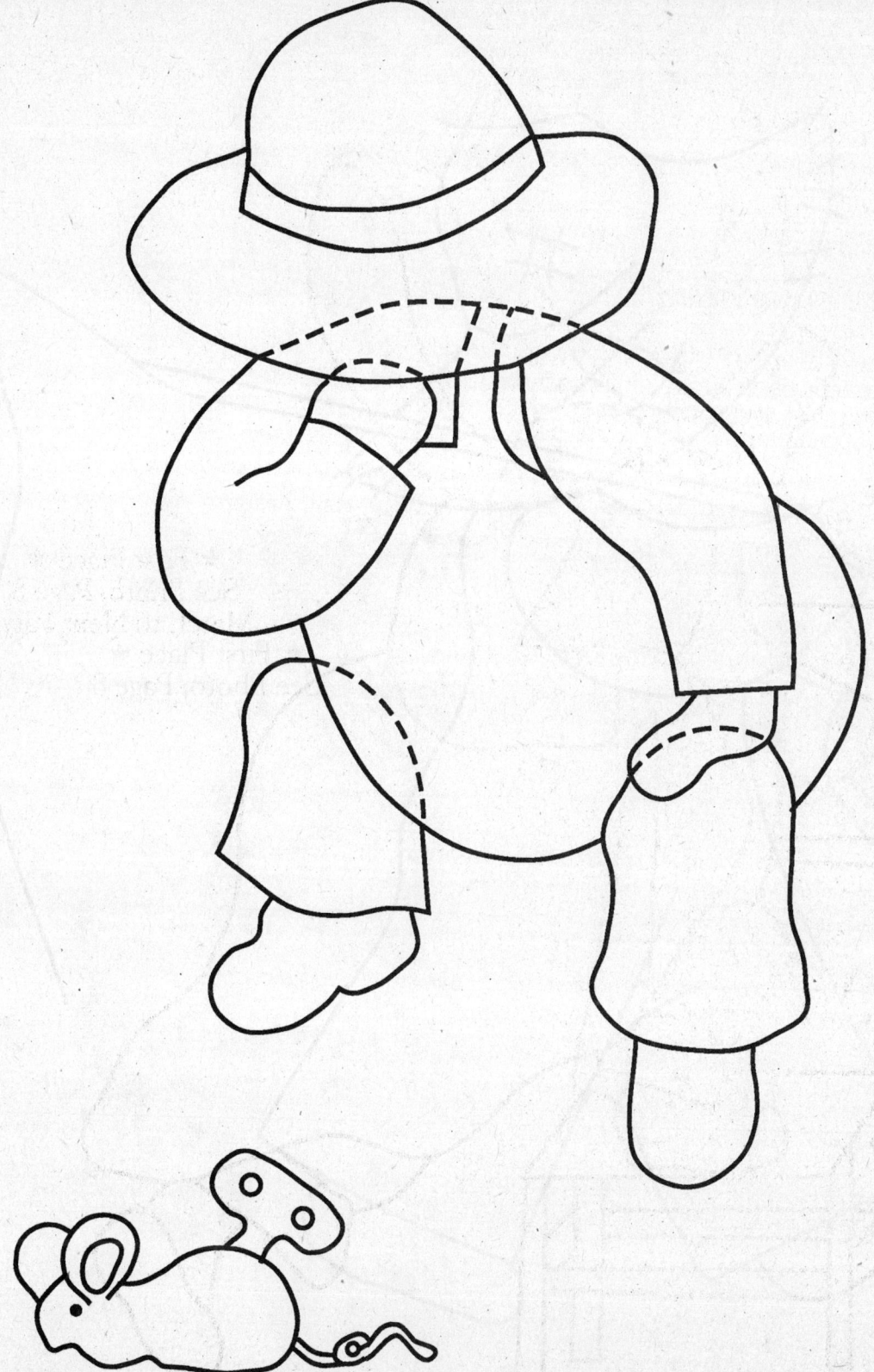

Sunbonnet Family Reunion

Sunbonnet FAMILY REUNION

Sam Goes Fishing
Esther Weisser • Tripp, SD

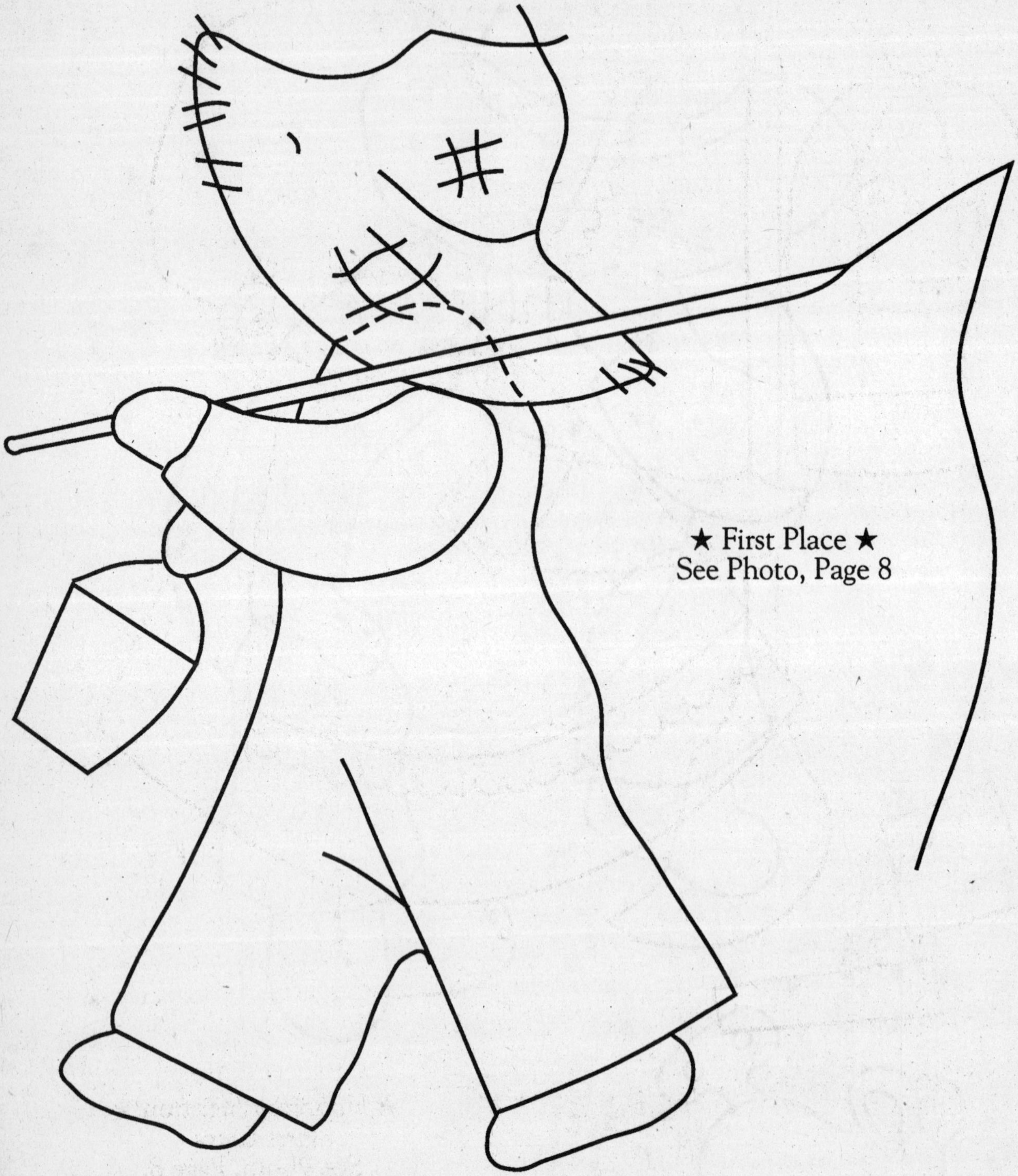

★ First Place ★
See Photo, Page 8

Sweeping Up Scraps
Elizabeth J. Prather • Grapevine, TX

Sunbonnet FAMILY REUNION

★ Honorary Mention ★
First Entry
See Photo, Page 8

Sunbonnet FAMILY REUNION

Come On Over & Play With Me
Pauline Loeffler • Inman, KS

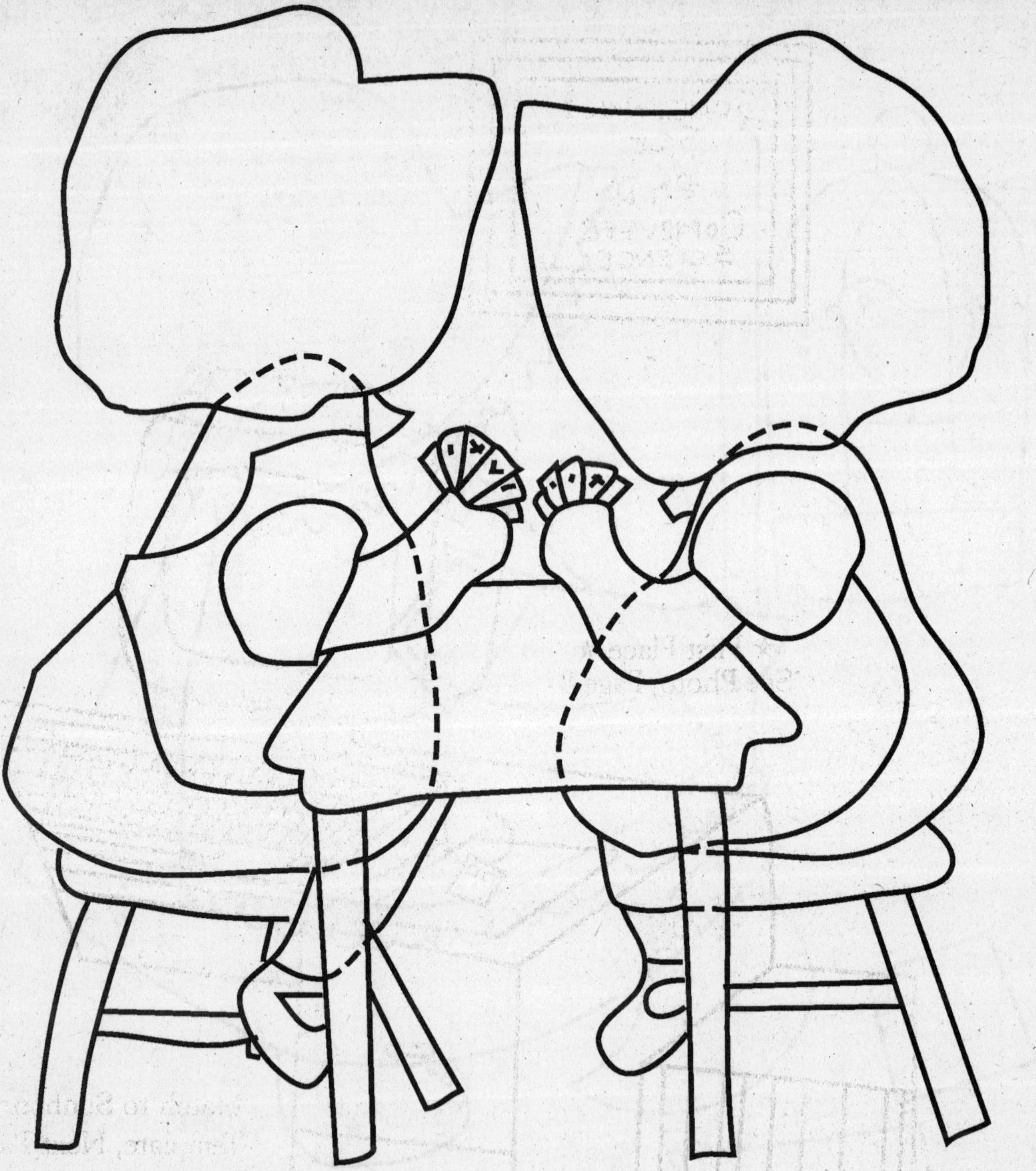

★ First Place ★
See Photo, Page 8

Come on over an play with me

44 Sunbonnet Family Reunion

Conquering The Computer Age
Sandra L. Christiansen • Phoenix, AZ

Sunbonnet FAMILY REUNION

★ First Place ★
See Photo, Page 8

Match to Sunbonnet
Template, Next Page

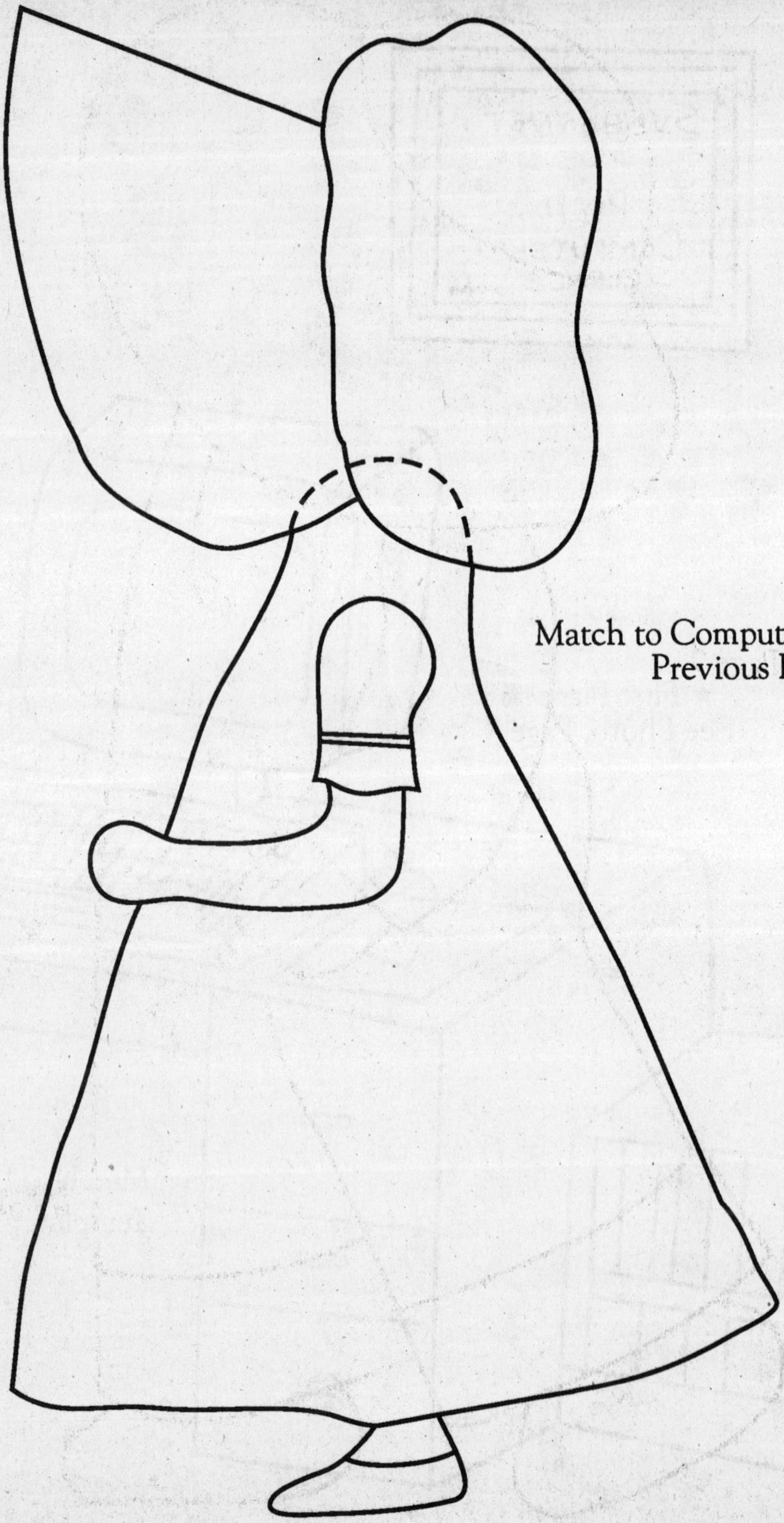

Match to Computer Template,
Previous Page

Overall Sam
Felicia Ryan • Newport News, VA

See Photo, Page 9

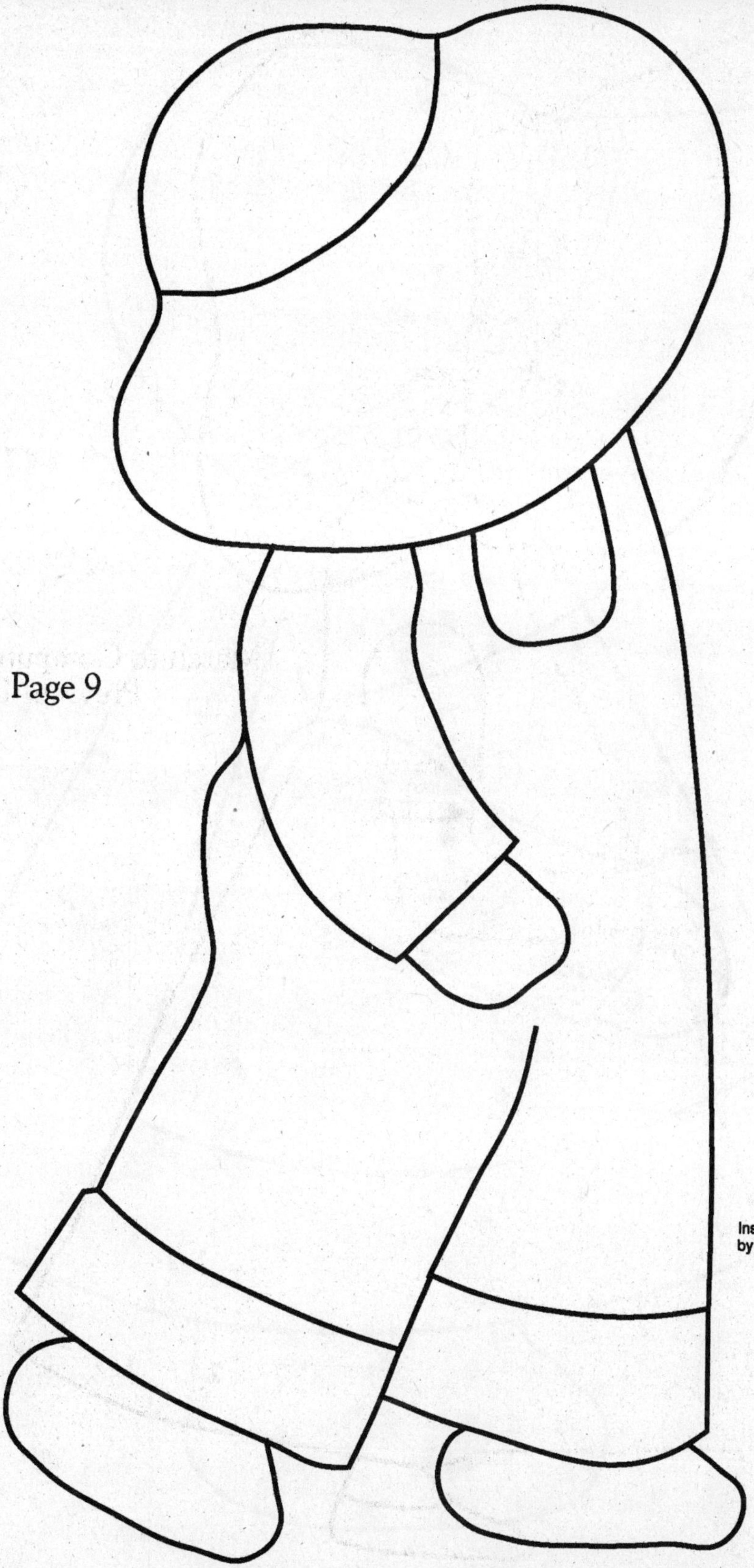

Inspired by *Country Children* by Pat Cox

Sunbonnet Sue
Tammie Nisbilt • Dimmit, TX

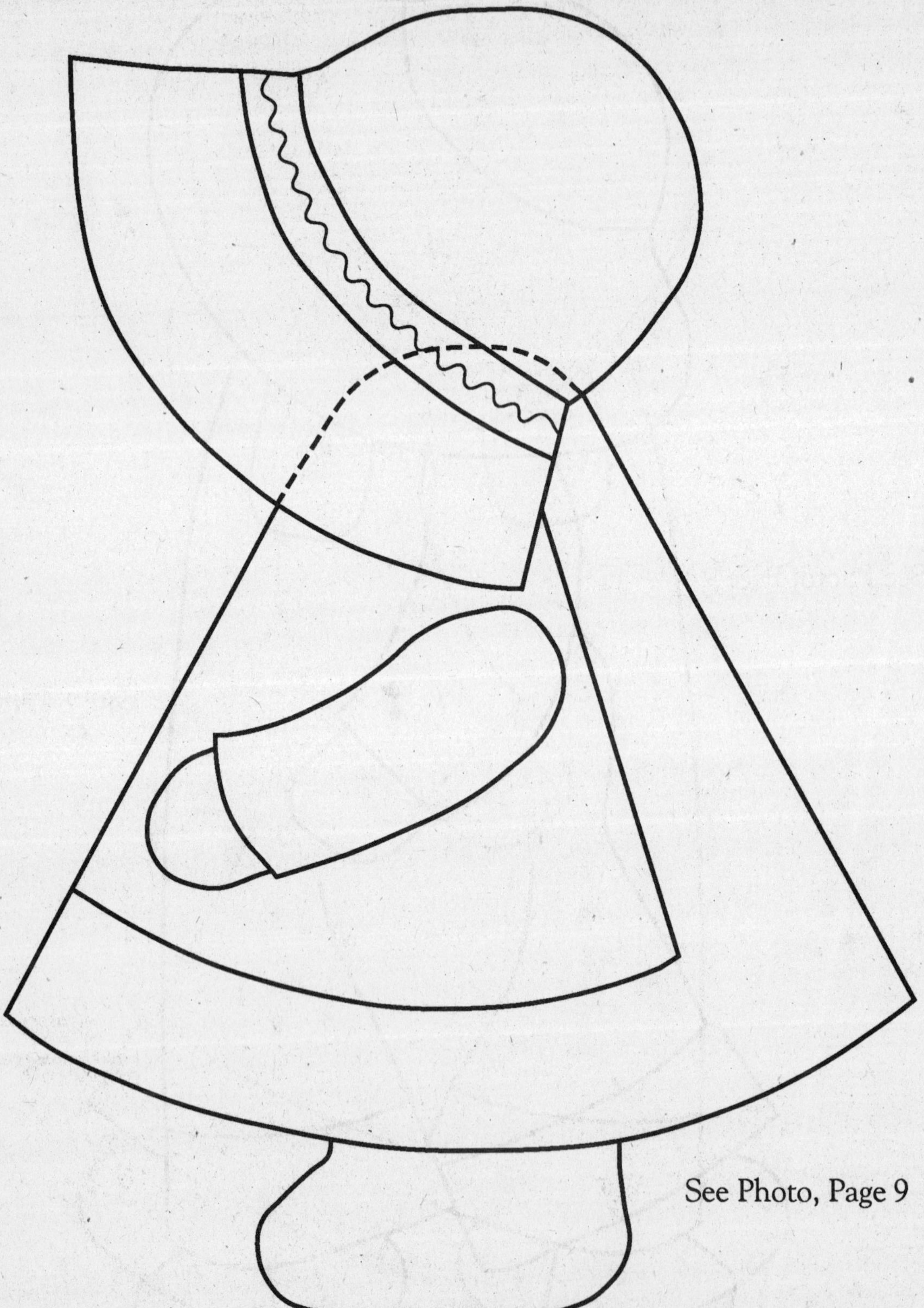

See Photo, Page 9

Overall Sam
Felicia Ryan • Newport News, VA

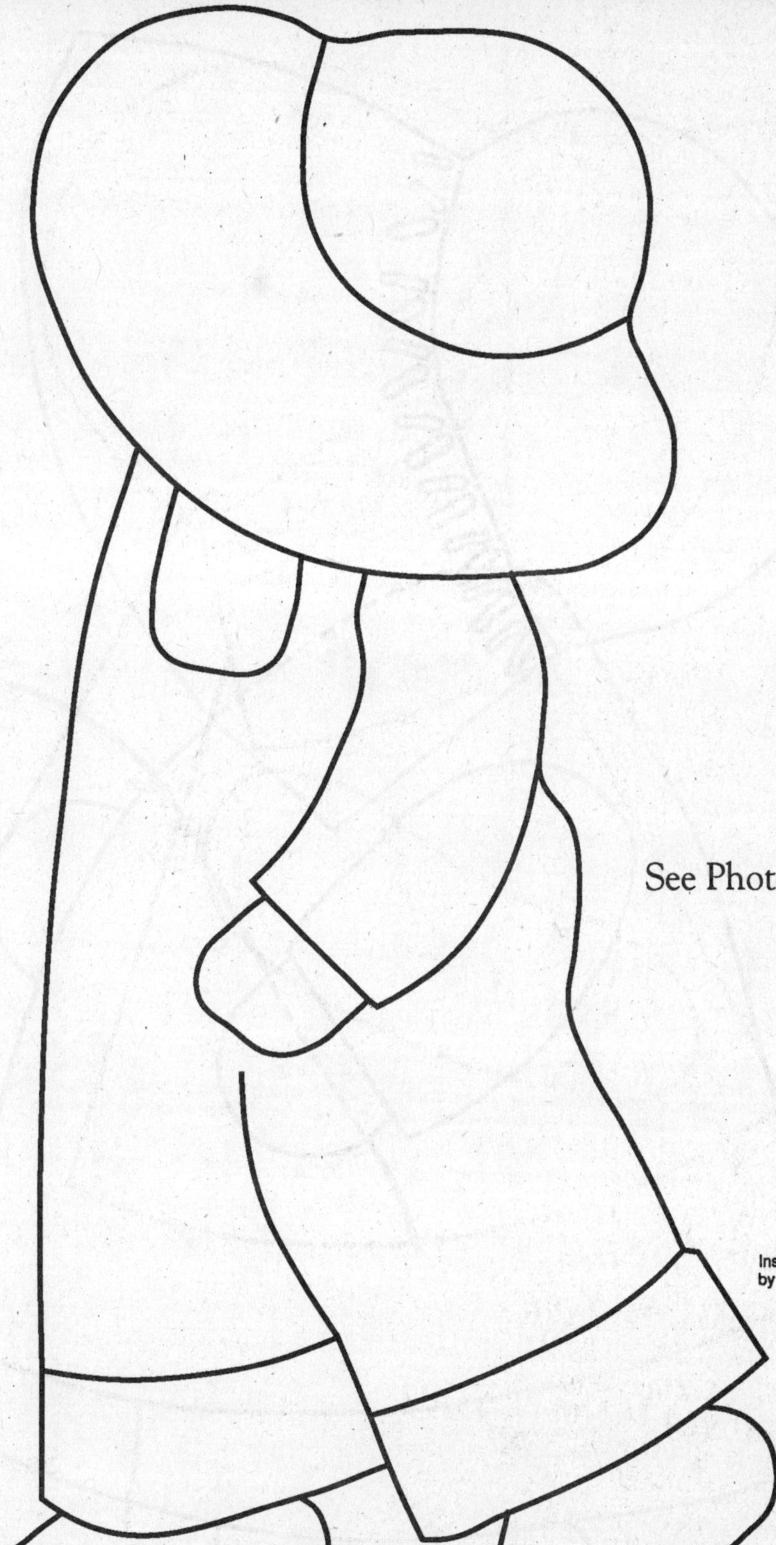

See Photo, Page 9

Inspired by *Country Children* by Pat Cox

Traditional Sunbonnet
Marian S. Woods • Central City, IA

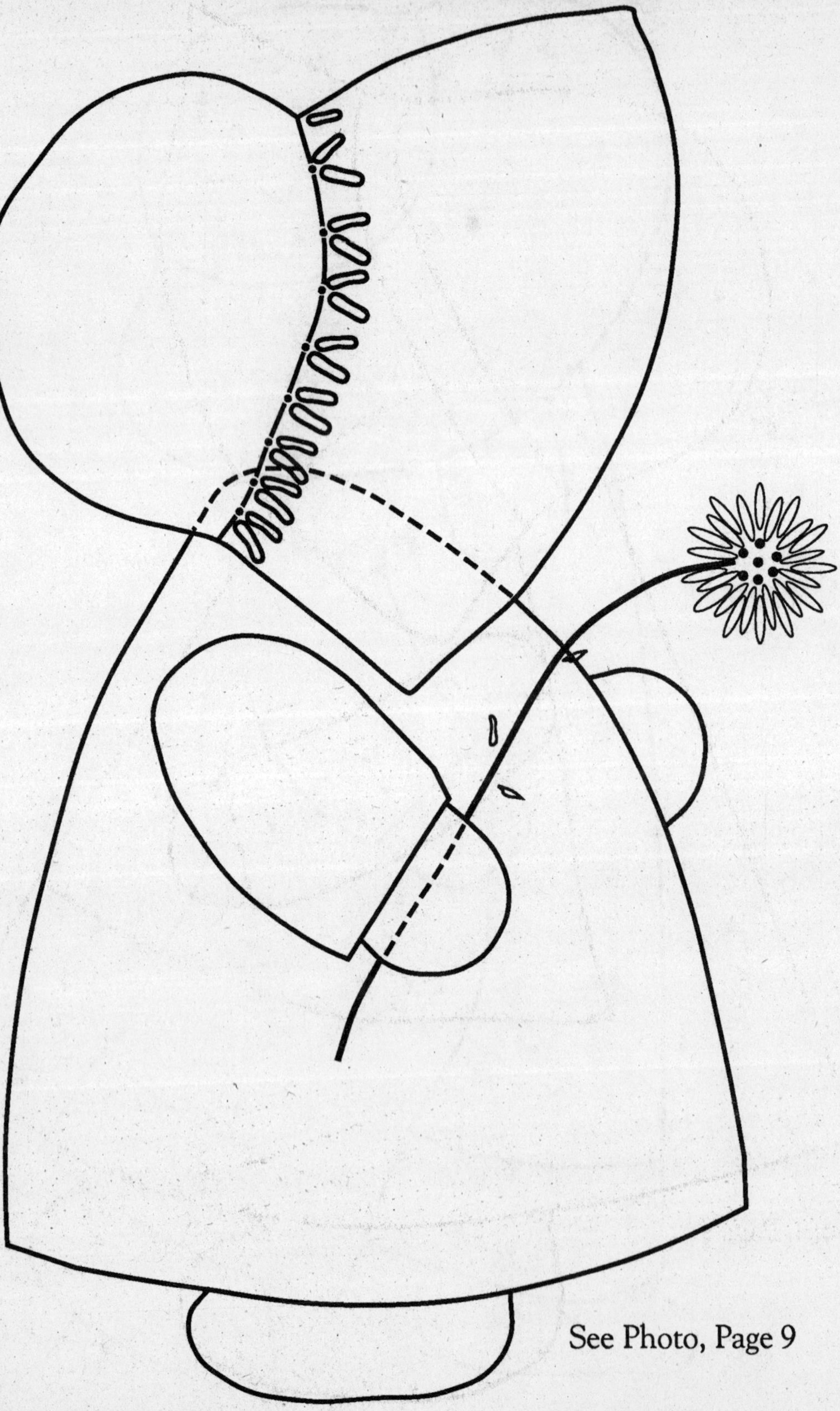

See Photo, Page 9

Texas Sunbonnet Sue
Doris Lust • Dimmit, TX

Sunbonnet FAMILY REUNION

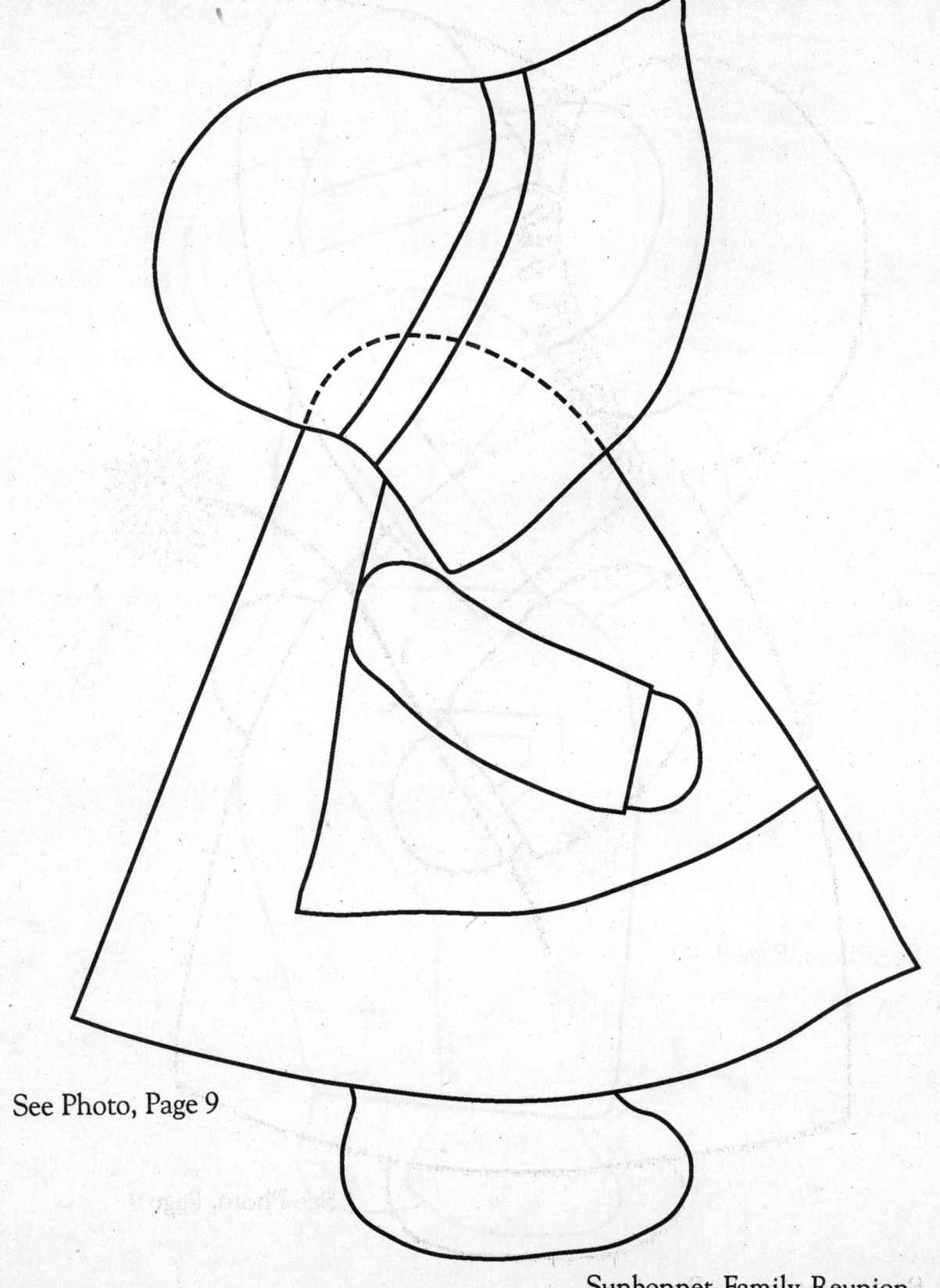

See Photo, Page 9

Sunbonnet Family Reunion

Texas Overall Bill
Doris Lust • Dimmit, TX

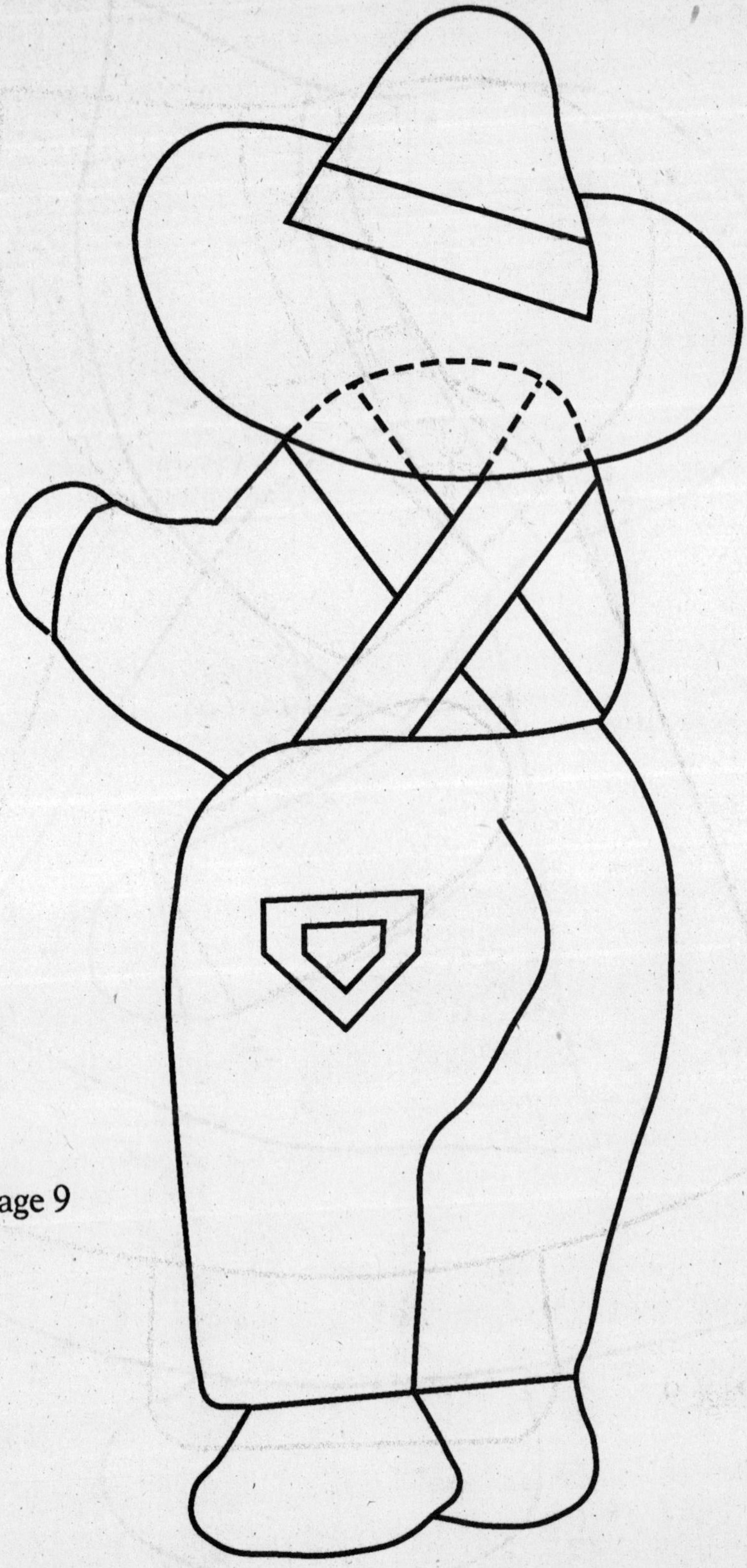

See Photo, Page 9

52 Sunbonnet Family Reunion

Mom's Sunbonnet Sue 1939-1989
Carrie Mae Gehrke • Libby, MT

See Photo, Page 9

Sunbonnet Family Reunion 53

Texas Sunbonnet Sue
Oma Dee Heard • Dimmitt, TX

See Photo, Page 9

Sunbonnet Sue
Nell Humphrey • Dimmitt, TX

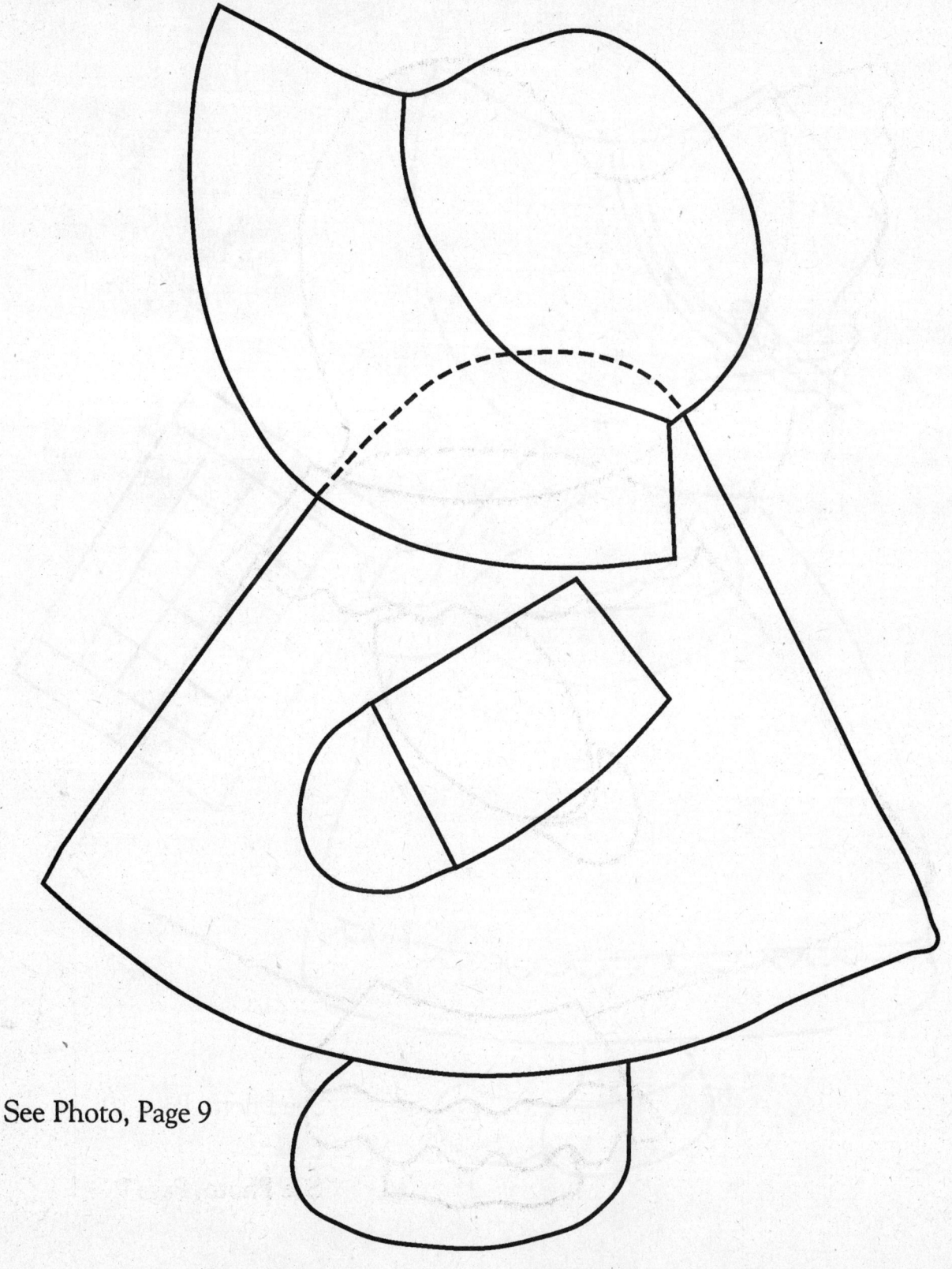

See Photo, Page 9

Sue Has A Quilt
Barbara Alexcites • Lenexa, KS

See Photo, Page 10

Quilting
Helen Siegel • New Port Richey, FL

Sunbonnet FAMILY REUNION

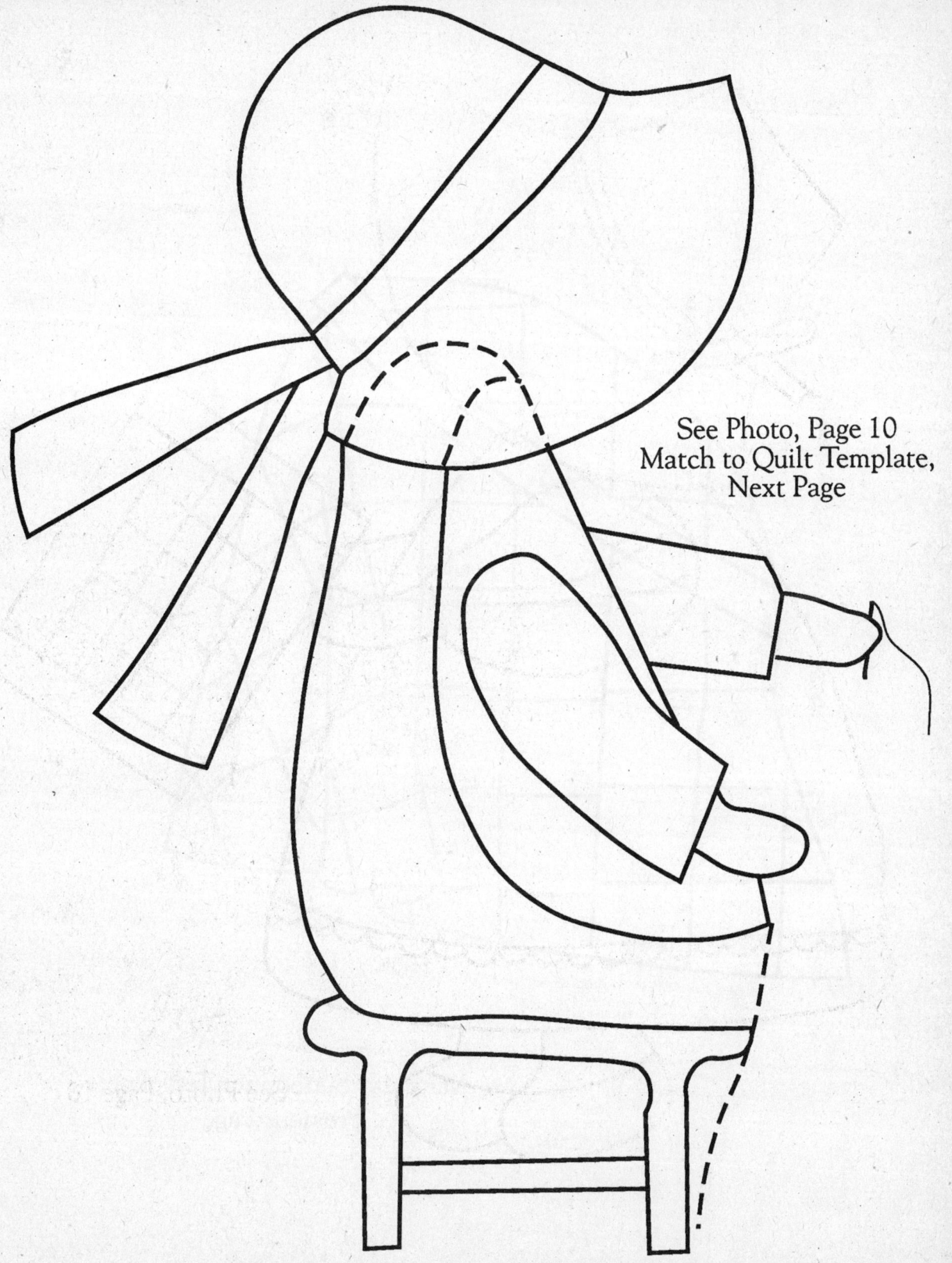

See Photo, Page 10
Match to Quilt Template, Next Page

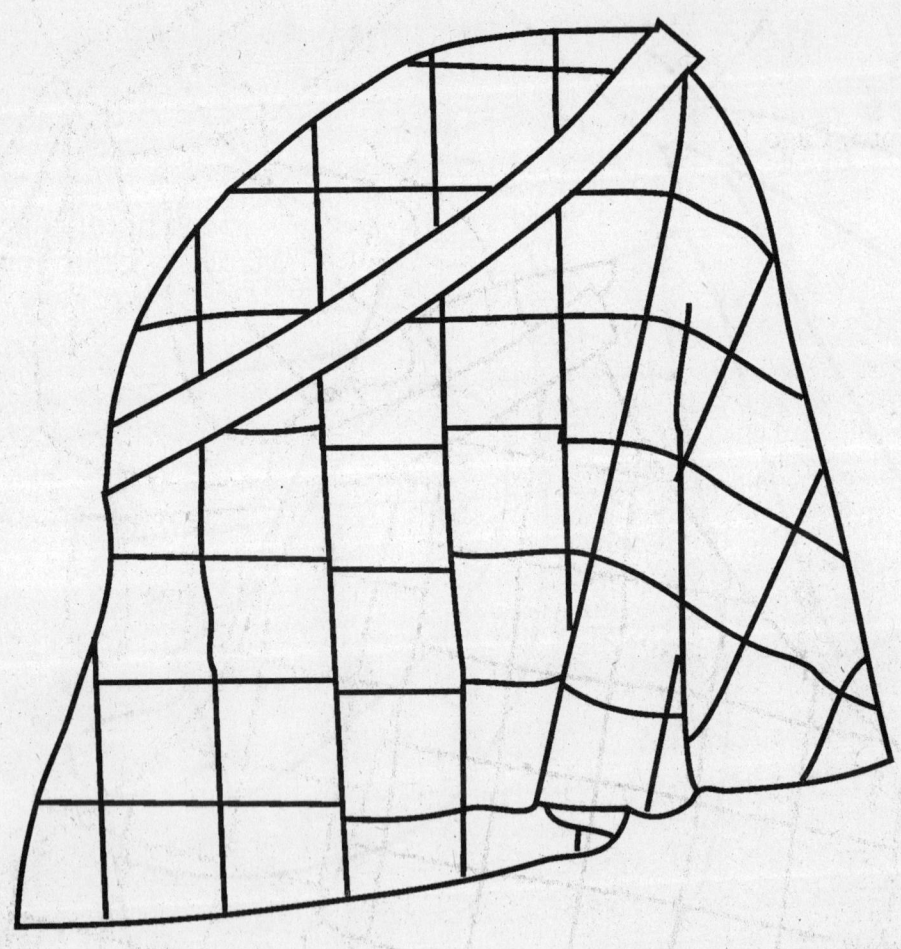

Match to Sunbonnet Template,
Previous Page

58 Sunbonnet Family Reunion

Little Miss Quilter
Mary Jo Gussert • Greenleaf, WI

See Photo, Page 10

Pattern adapted from *The Magical Unicorn*

Gone Fishin'
Irma K. Kendall • Hollandale, MS

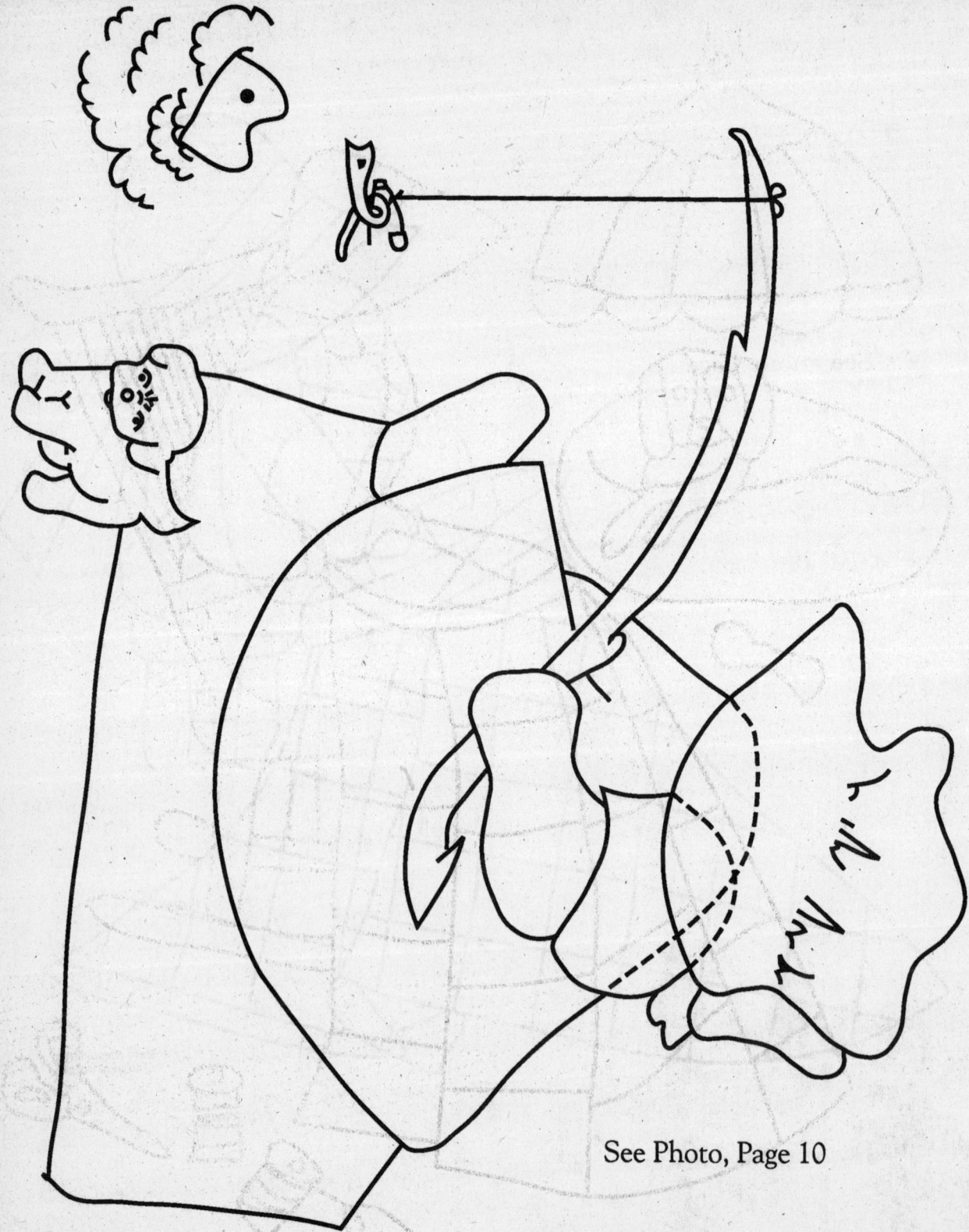

See Photo, Page 10

Quiet Night
Setsako T. O'Neill • Wyoming, MI

See Photo, Page 10

Always A Bridesmaid
Betty Boyink • Grand Haven, MI

See Photo, Page 10

Rocking-Chair Quilter
Ruth Starkey • Pineville, LA

See Photo, Page 10

Just Quilting
Dixie D. Moody • Yale, OK

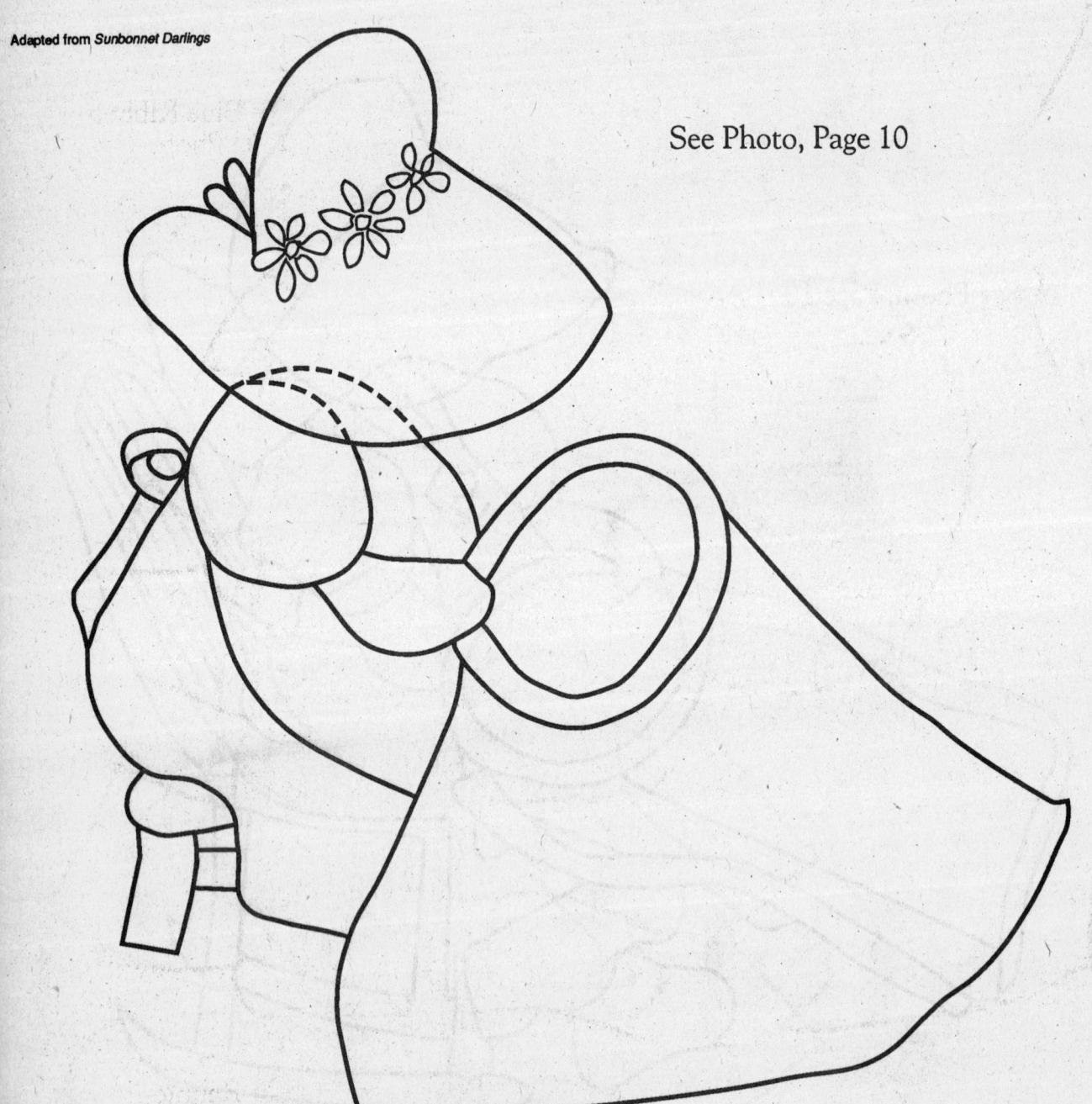

Adapted from *Sunbonnet Darlings*

See Photo, Page 10

My Quilt
Geneva Dunster • Atchison, KS

Adapted from *Sunbonnet Children* by Betty Hagerman

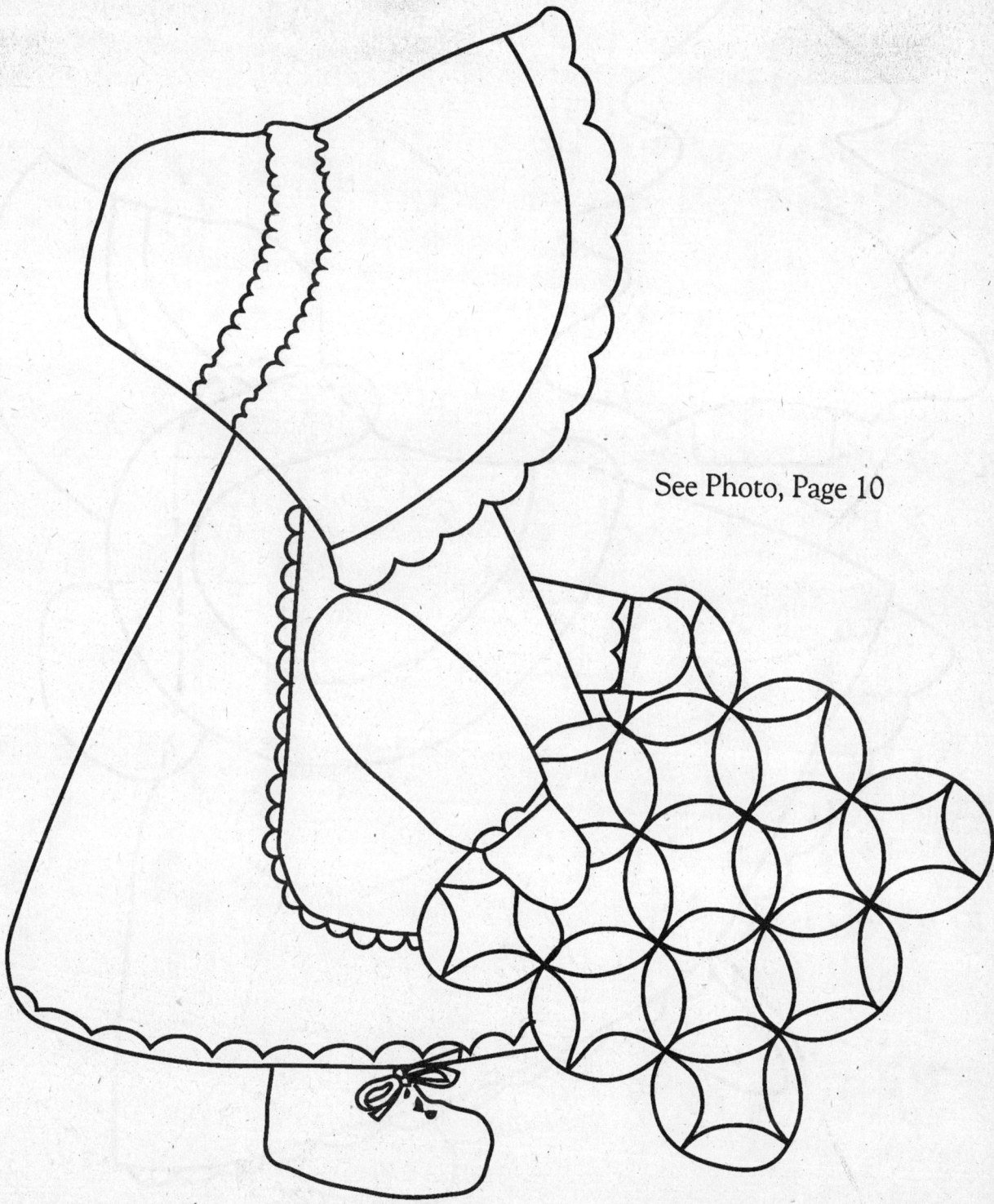

See Photo, Page 10

Sunbonnet FAMILY REUNION

Ice-Skating
Mickey K. Geismar • Gonzales, LA

Adapted from *Stitch 'N Sew Quilt's Calander Quilt* © Edie Haynie

See Photo, Page 11

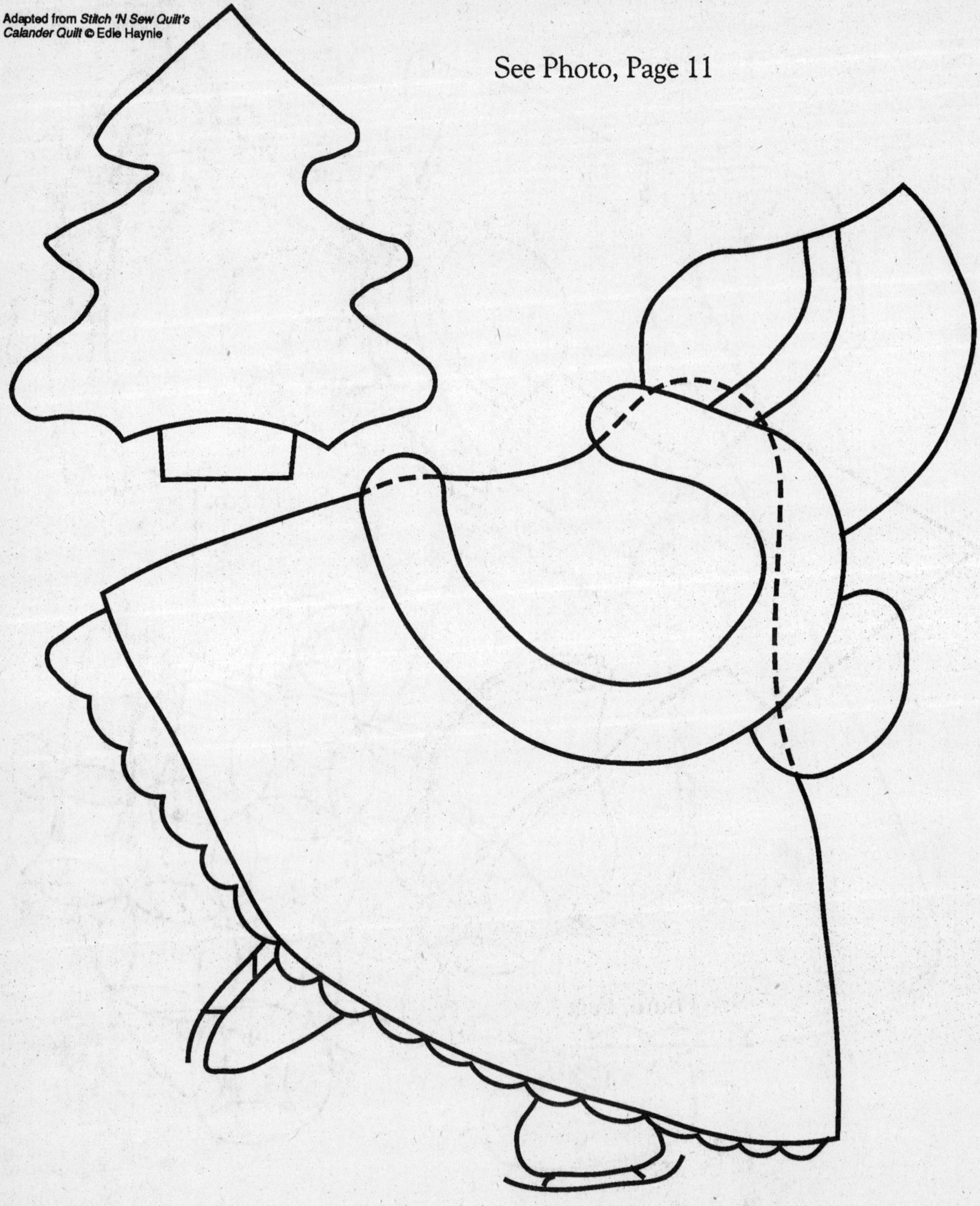

Help Us Trim The Tree
Annadell Teems • Granbury, TX

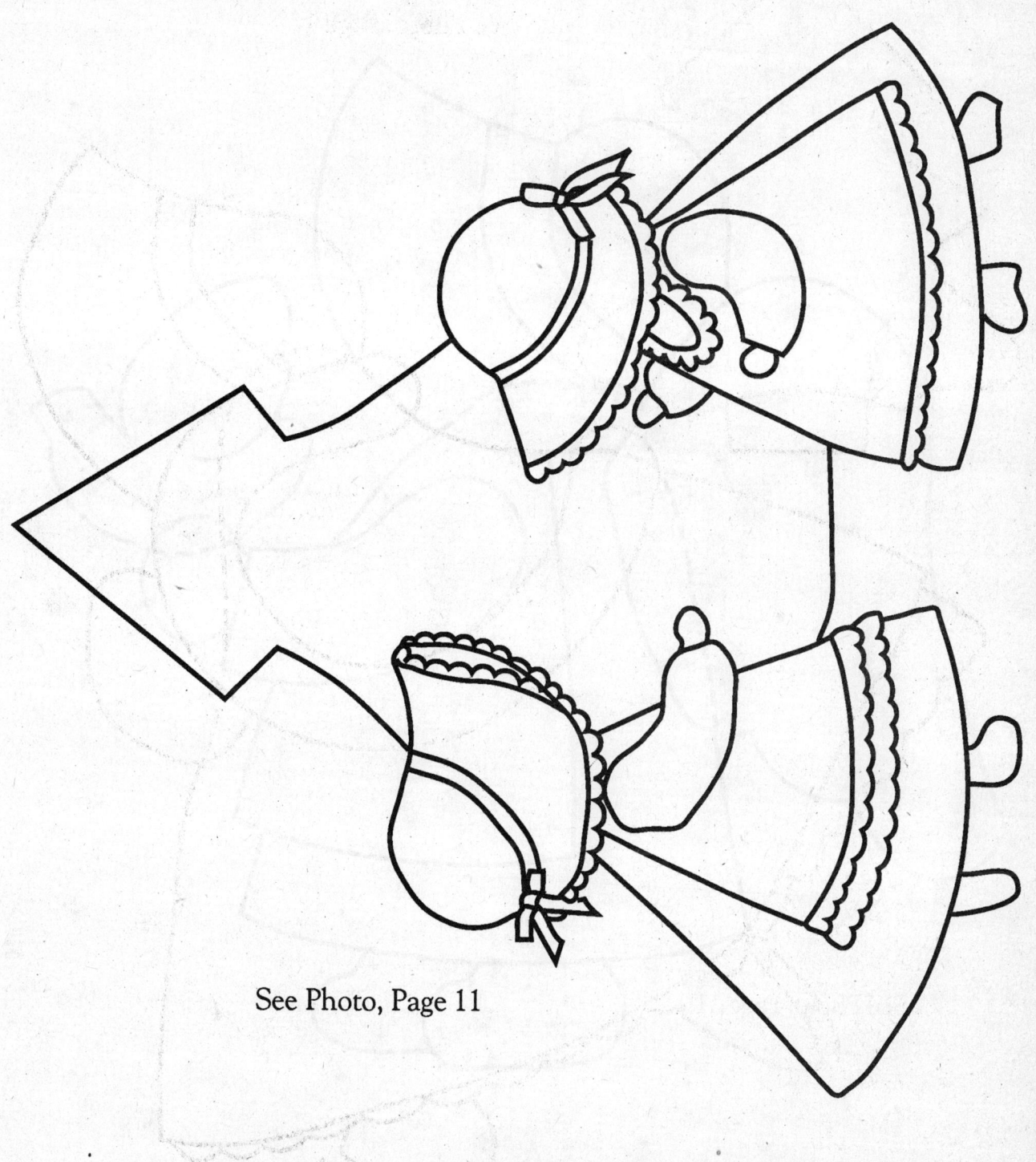

See Photo, Page 11

Sunbonnet FAMILY REUNION

Christmastime
Lavona Keltner • Camdenton, MO

See Photo, Page 11

Teddy Bear Security
Claudia Brownfield • Aspermont, TX

Sunbonnet FAMILY REUNION

See Photo, Page 11

Mary Christmas
Sandra Andrews • Medina, OH

Adapted from *Sunbonnet Family of Quilts* by Delores Hinson

See Photo, Page 11

Skating Sunbonnet
Irene Sliwinski • Keene, NH

Adapted from Edie Haynie

See Photo, Page 11

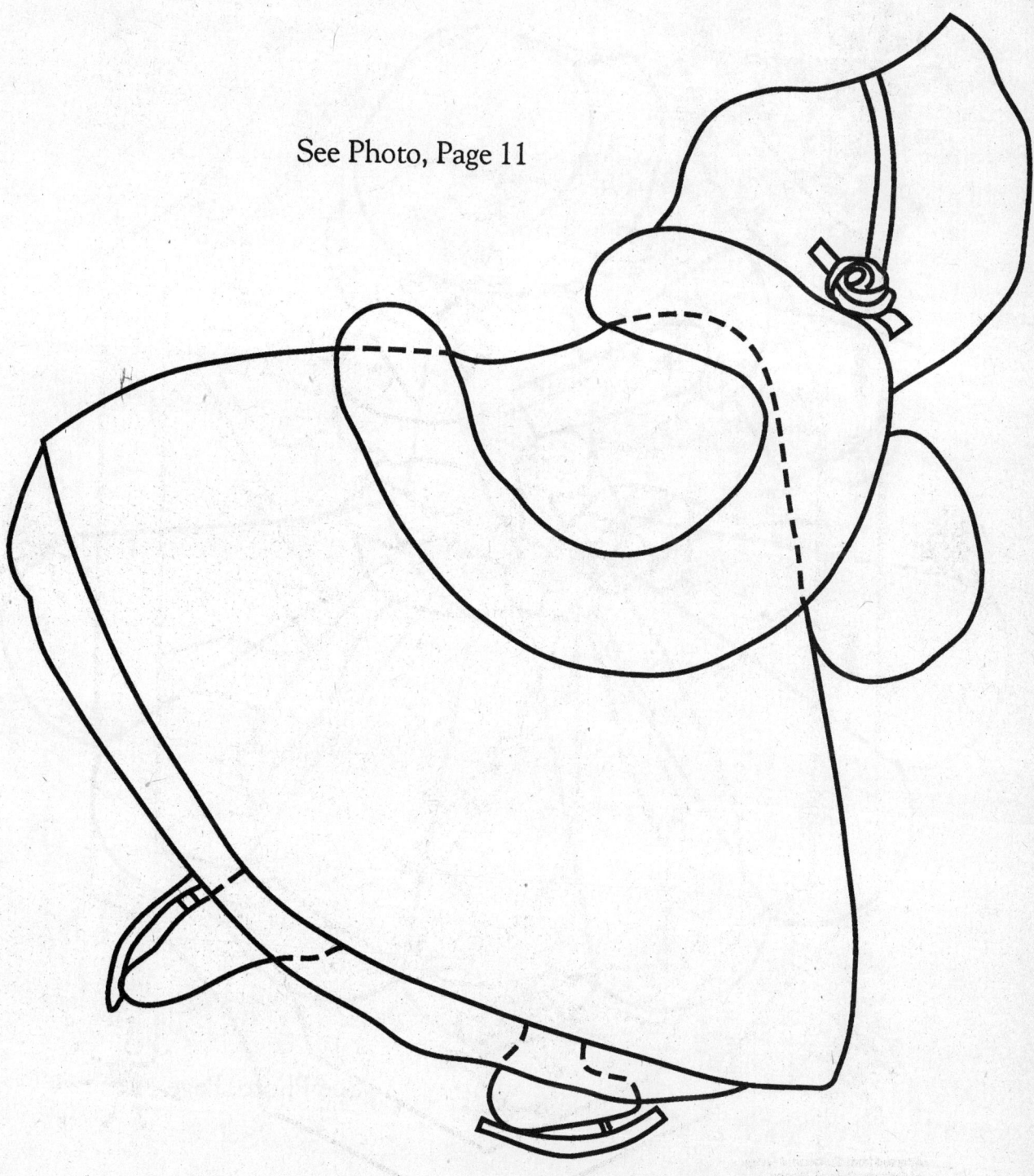

Sunbonnet Family Reunion 71

Sunbonnet Family Reunion — Me & Sunny In Our Sunday Dresses
Linda Elaine Crowell • Greenville, OH

See Photo, Page 11

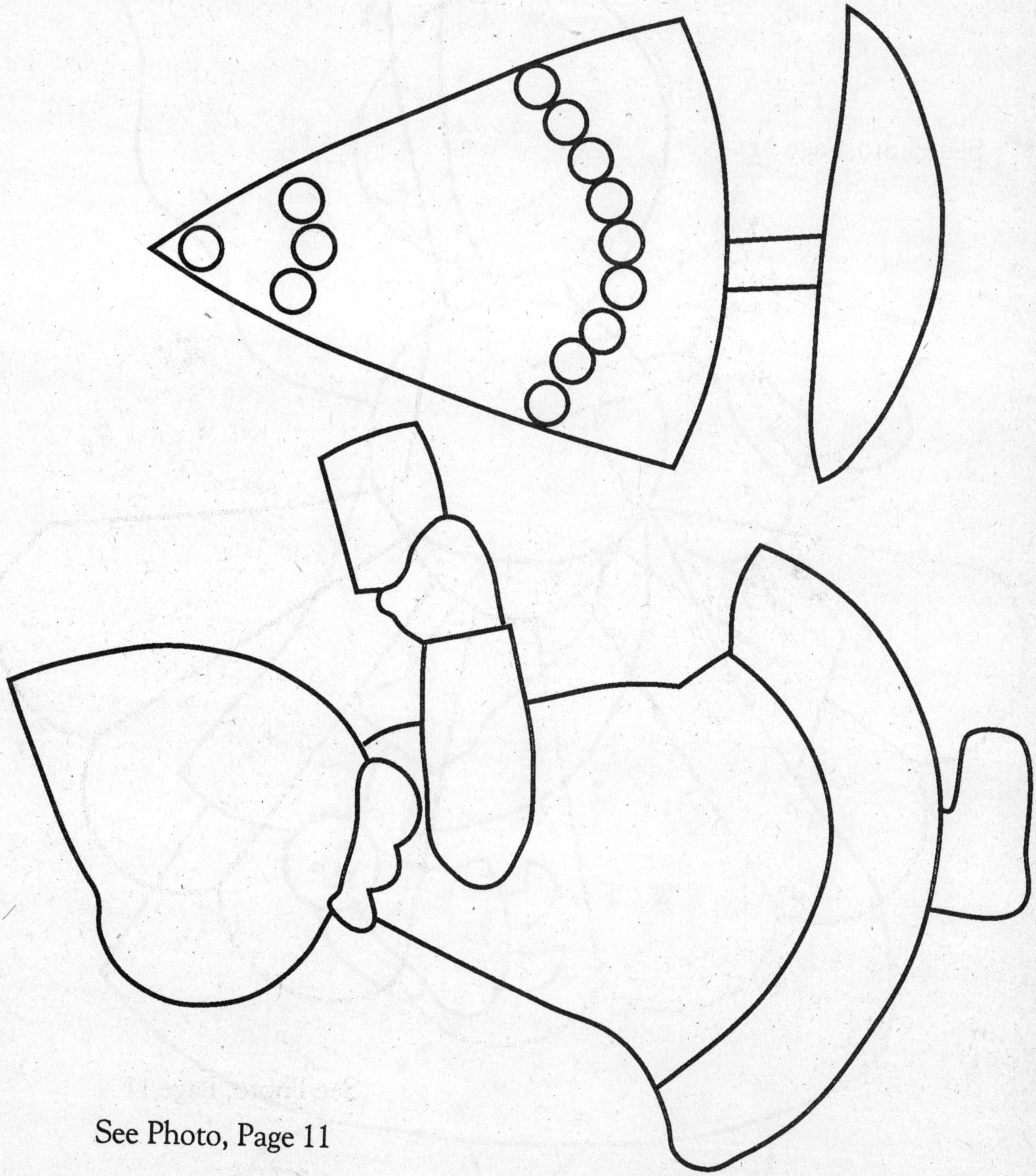

A Christmas Present
Alta Rymer • Clovis, CA

See Photo, Page 11

Sunbonnet Sue & Doll
Lee Streib • Pleasant Hill, CA

See Photo, Page 11

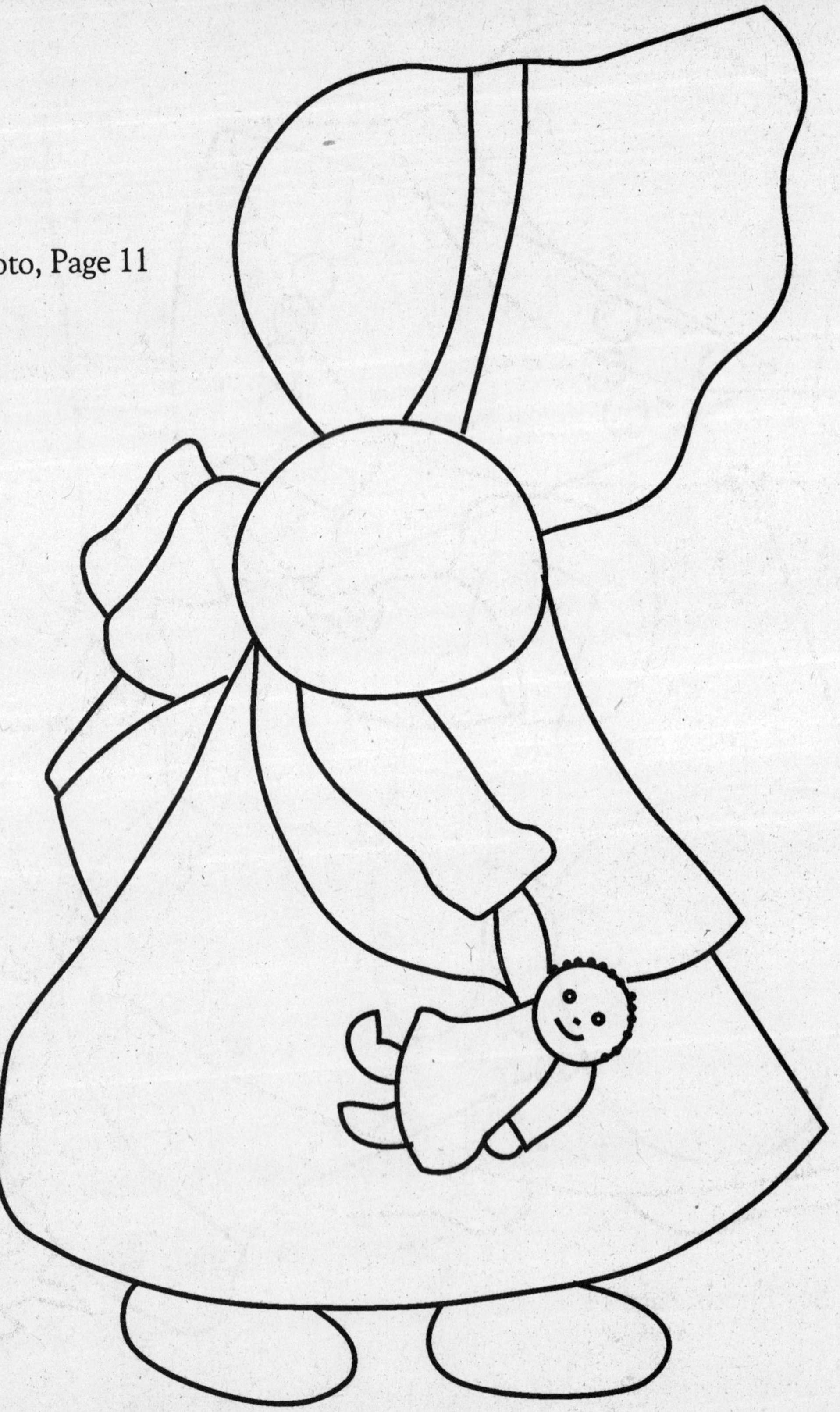

Paper Dolls For Sue
Sue Moore • Tulsa, OK

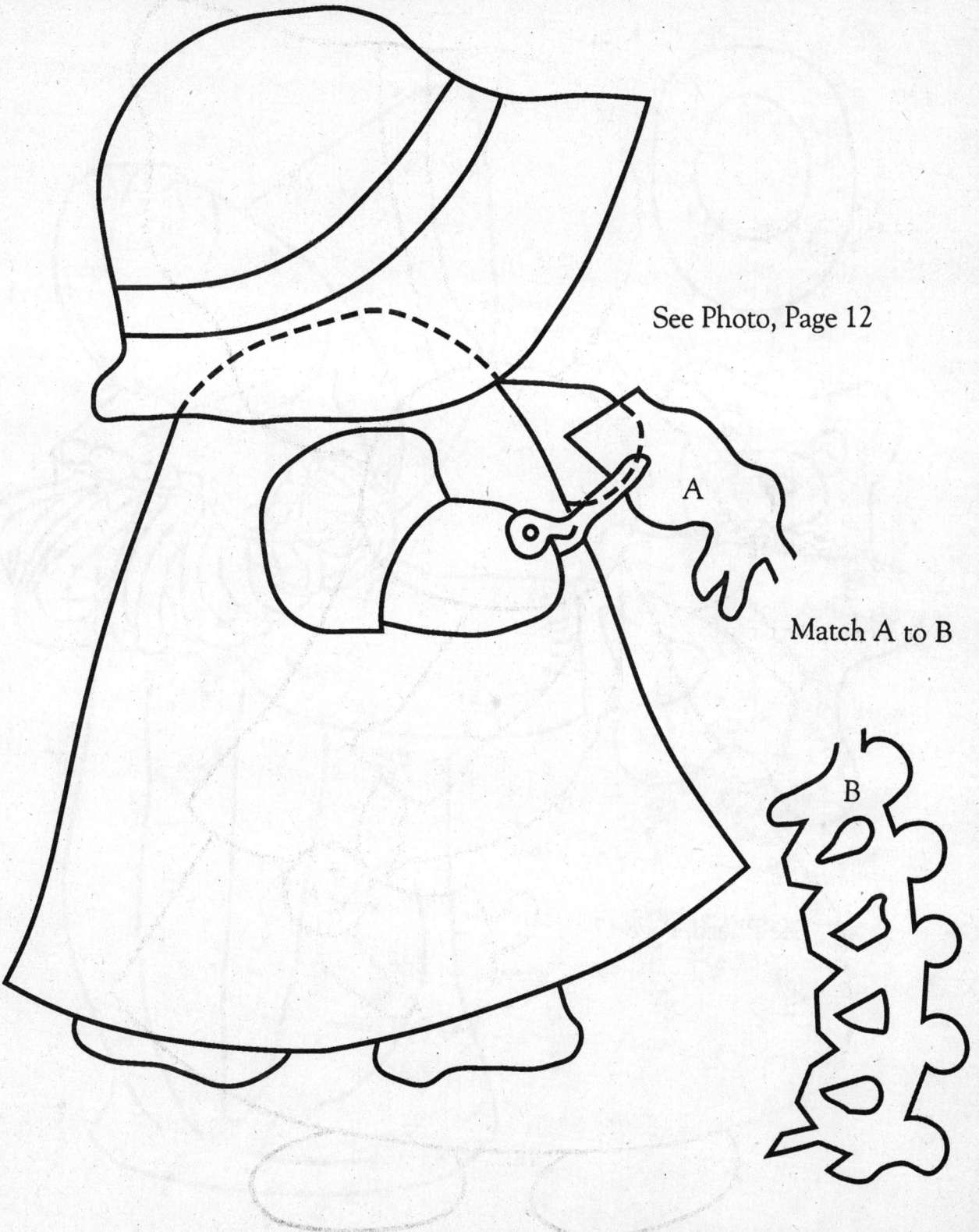

See Photo, Page 12

Match A to B

Sunbonnet Family Reunion

Sunbonnet FAMILY REUNION

Playing With My Teddy Bear
Susan L. McMullin • Sunnyside, WA

See Photo, Page 12

Going To Grandma's House
Mrs. George A. Richard • Emporia, KS

See Photo, Page 12

Sue & Her Doll
Ida Mae Drommer • Norton, KS

See Photo, Page 12

Shame On You, Sunbonnet Sue
June Wolpert • Nashville, IN

Match to Sunbonnet, Next Page
See Photo, Page 12

Sunbonnet Family Reunion 79

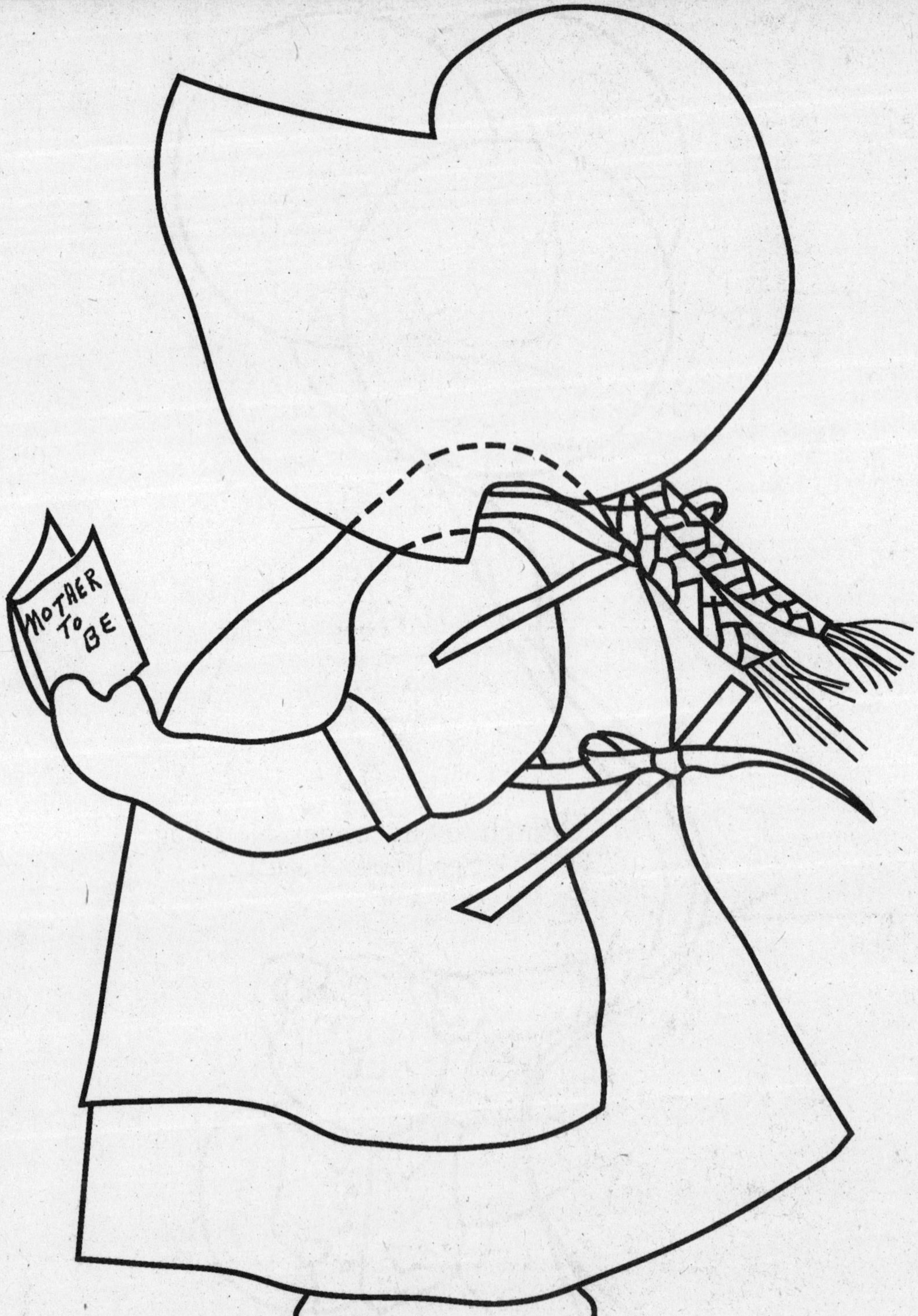

Match To Bear Template, Previous Page

Bedtime
Mary B. Mulligan • Abbotsford, B.C., Canada

Match with Sunbonnet
on Next Page
See Photo, Page 12

Sunbonnet Family Reunion

Match To Sunbonnet Template,
Previous Page

Tea Party
Sandra J. Heid • Cherokee, IA

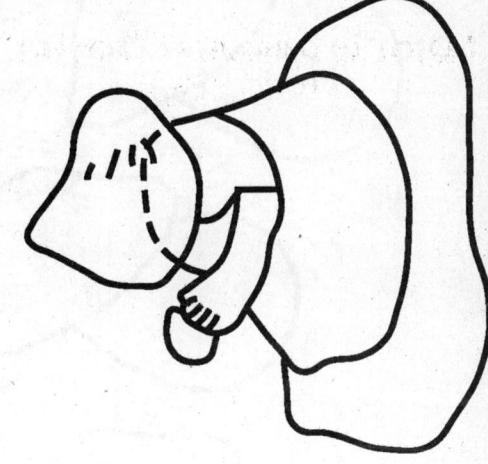

See Photo, Page 12

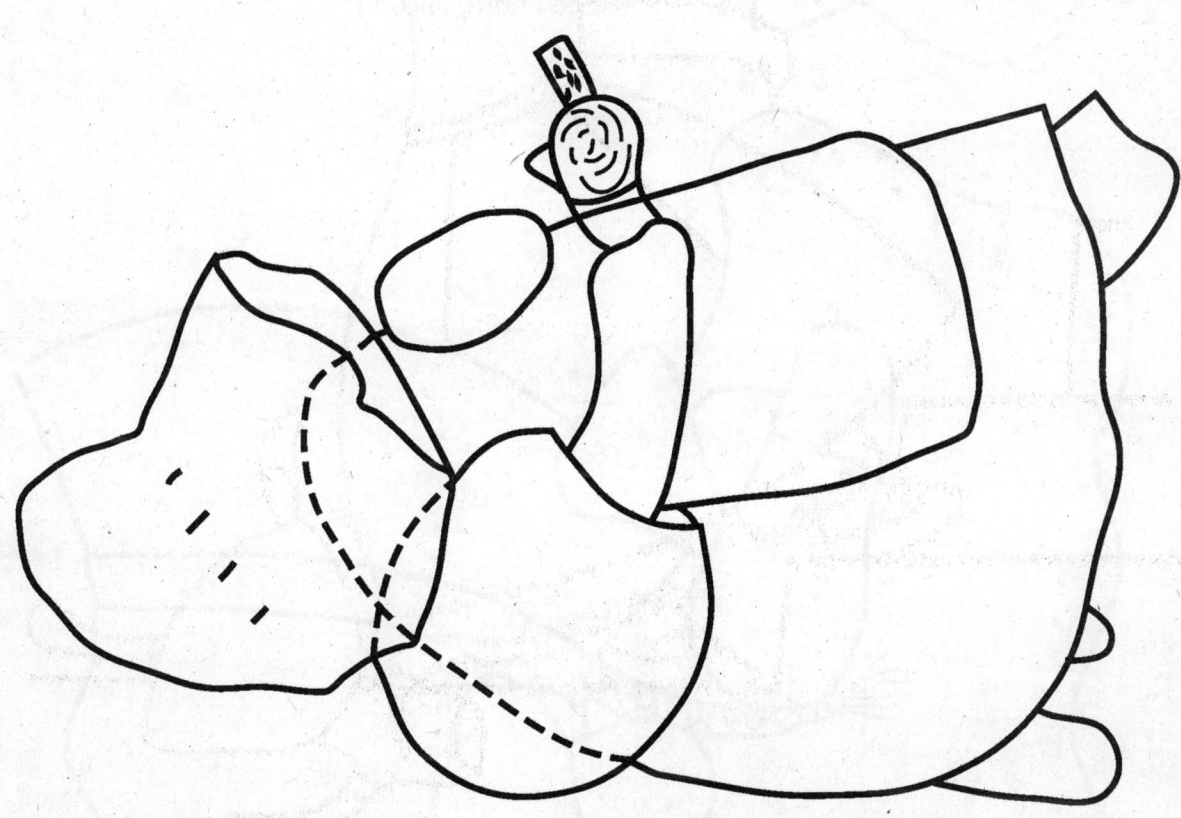

Sunbonnet Family Reunion

Storyteller Sue
Sandra Dick • Roswell, NM

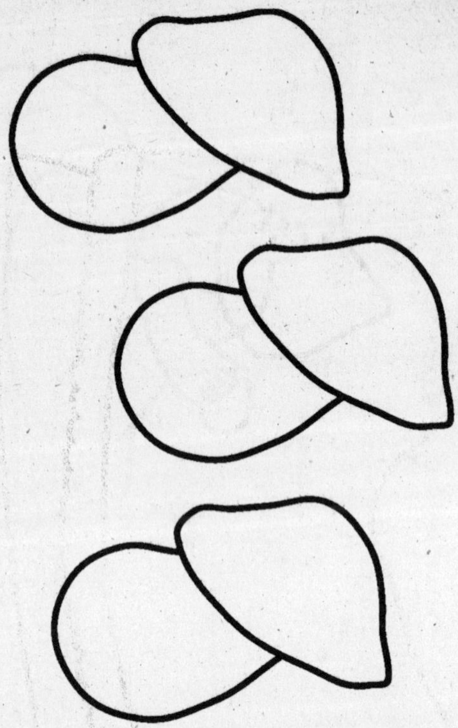

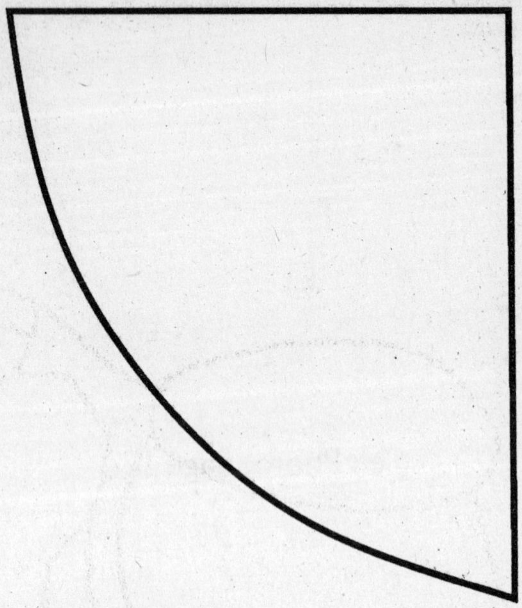

See Photo, Page 12

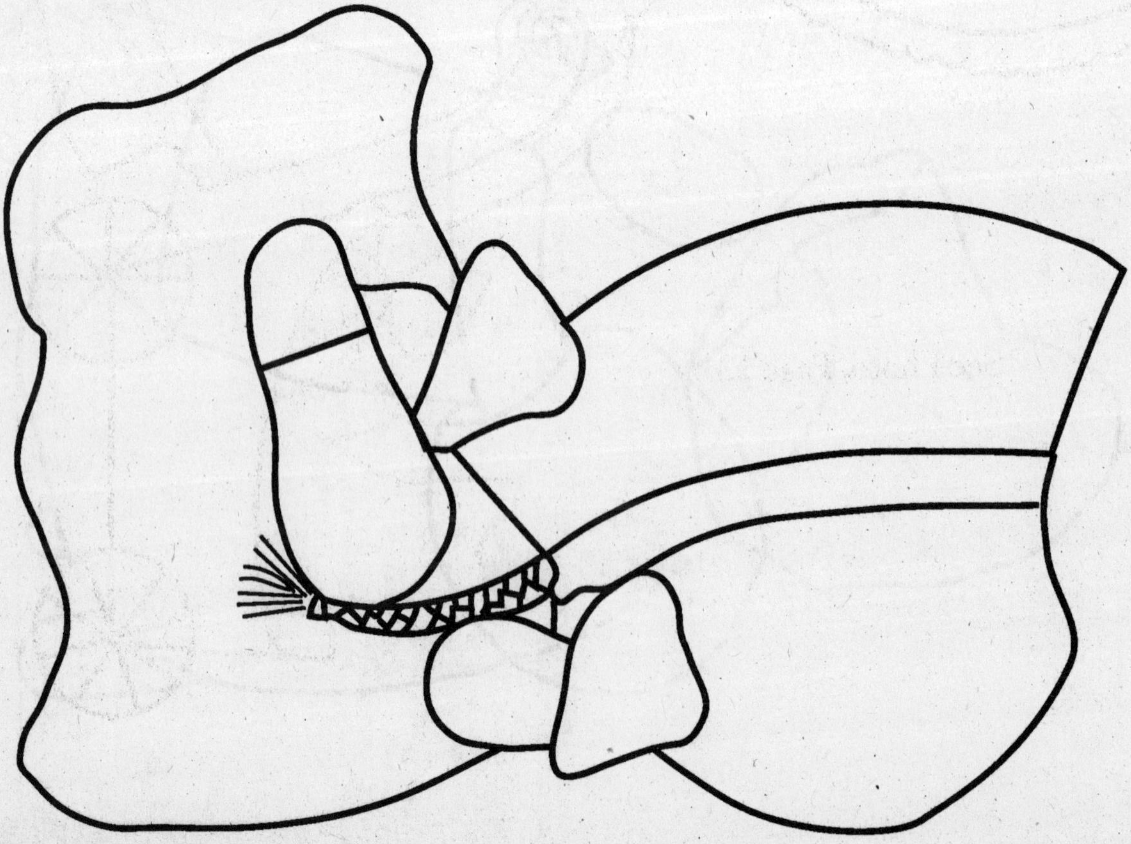

Going For A Walk
Sandra A. Anderson • Lincoln, NE

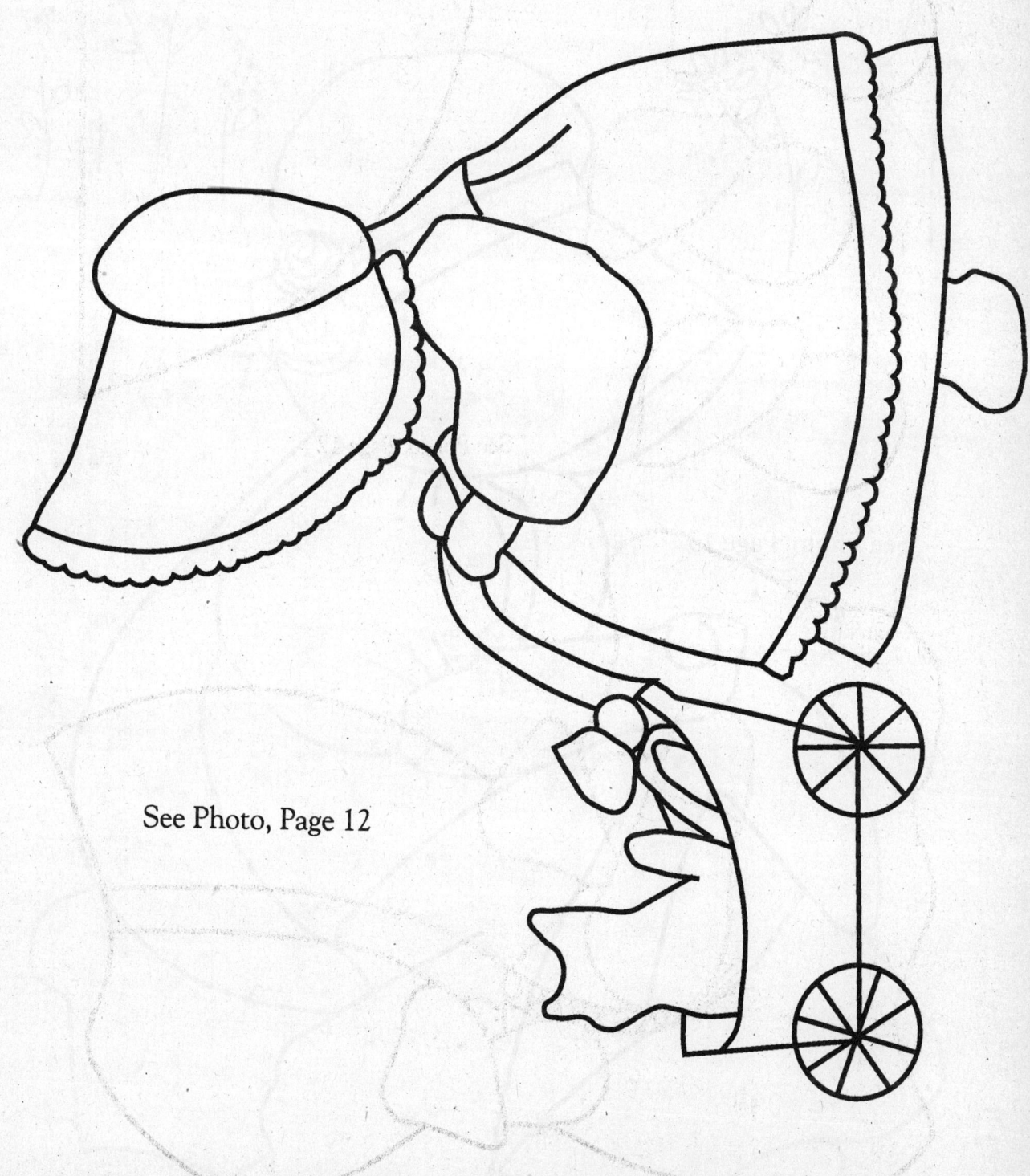

See Photo, Page 12

Sunbonnet FAMILY REUNION

Wednesday's Child
Maryon Peterson Ferguson • Eugene, OR

See Photo, Page 13

Fabrics For Her Next Quilt
Dolores M. Merle • Elmwood Park, IL

Sunbonnet FAMILY REUNION

See Photo, Page 13

Sunbonnet Family Reunion

Sue Goes To The Quilt Show
Leona E. Price • Florissant, MO

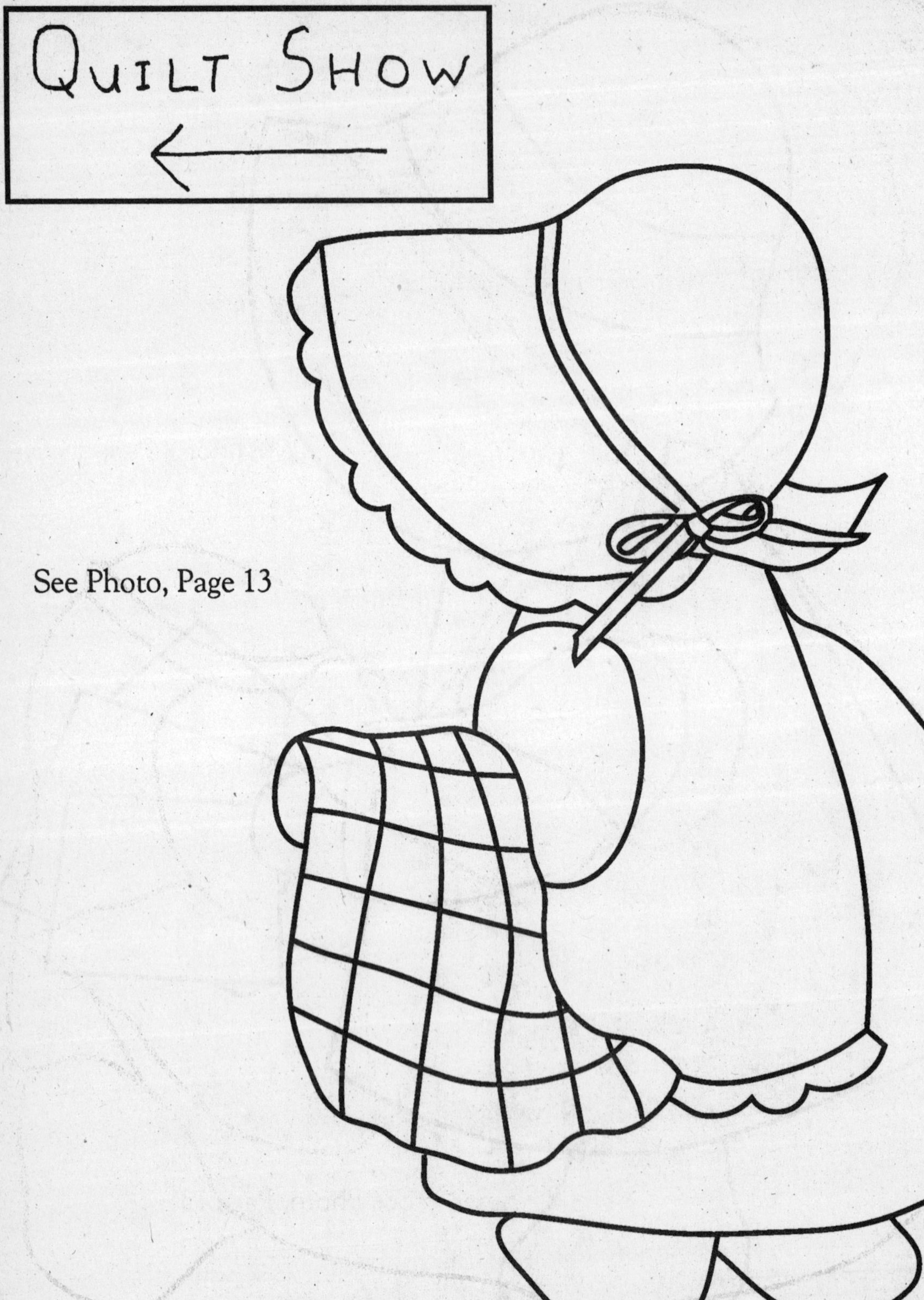

See Photo, Page 13

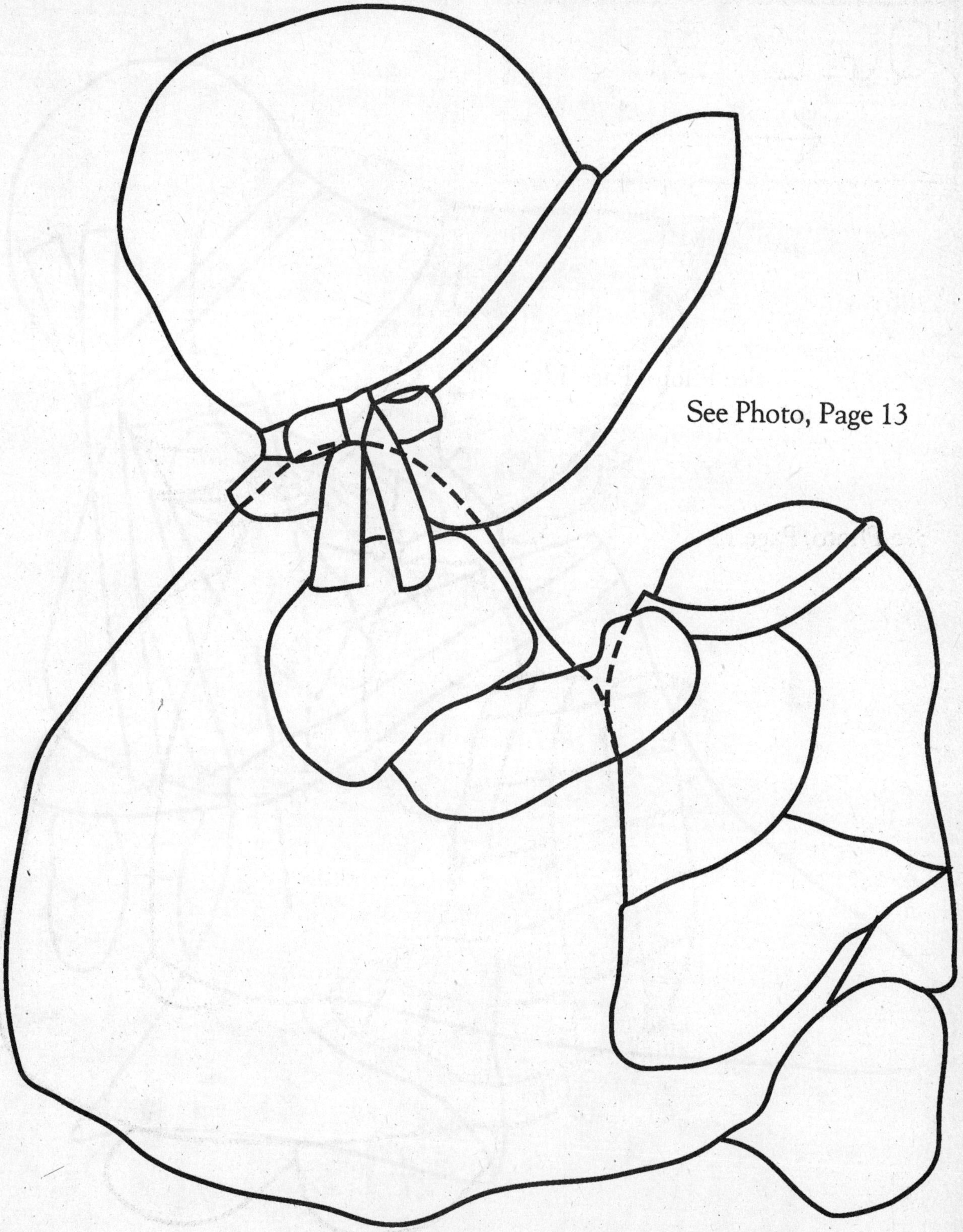

Making A Gift Of Love
Mary Ann Morris Newlon • St. Petersburg, FL

See Photo, Page 13

 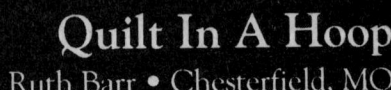

Quilt In A Hoop
Ruth Barr • Chesterfield, MO

See Photo, Page 13

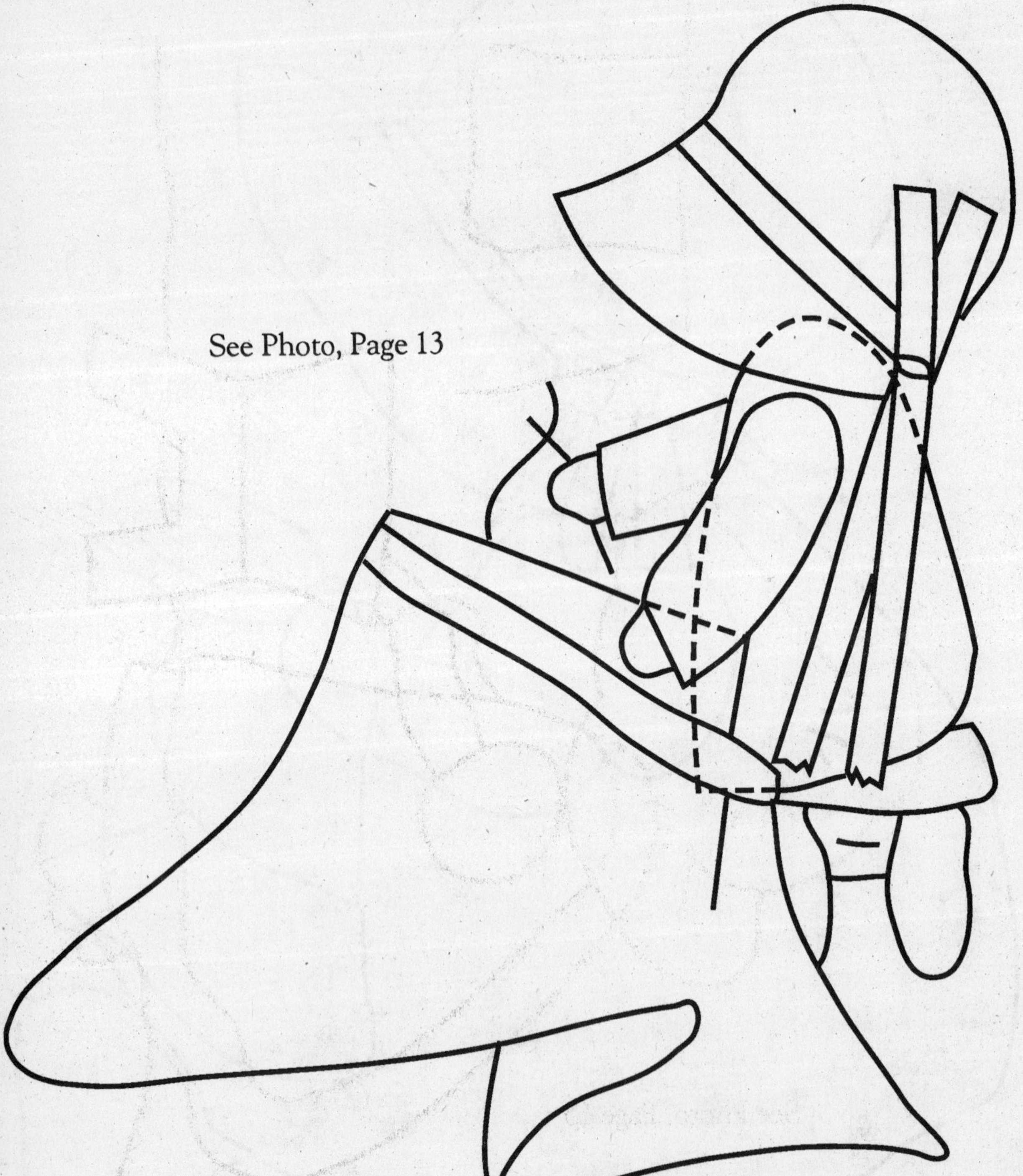

Laundry Day
Margaret Manti • Parma, OH

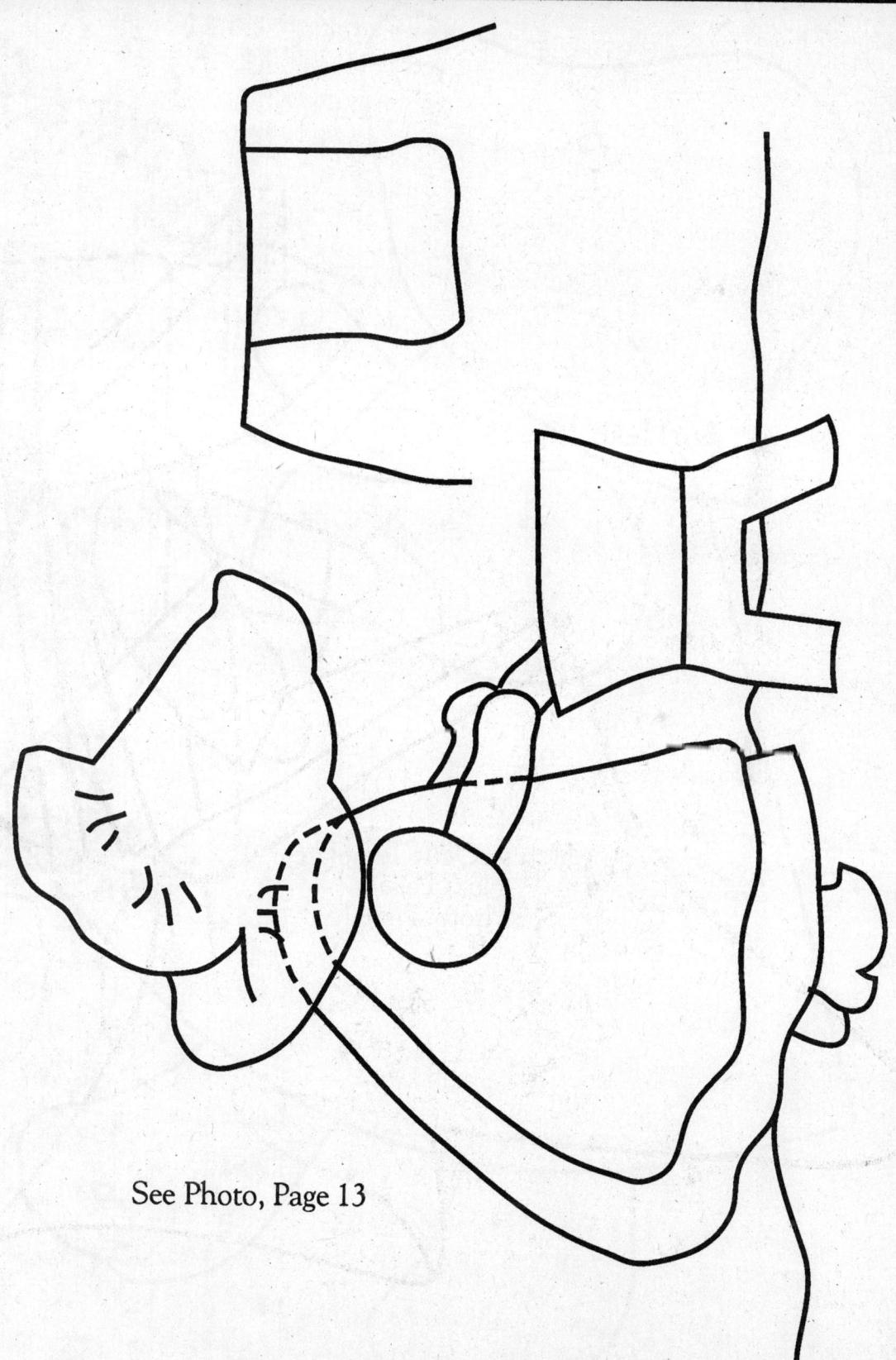

See Photo, Page 13

Airing Of The Day
Ann Sgro • Crystal River, FL

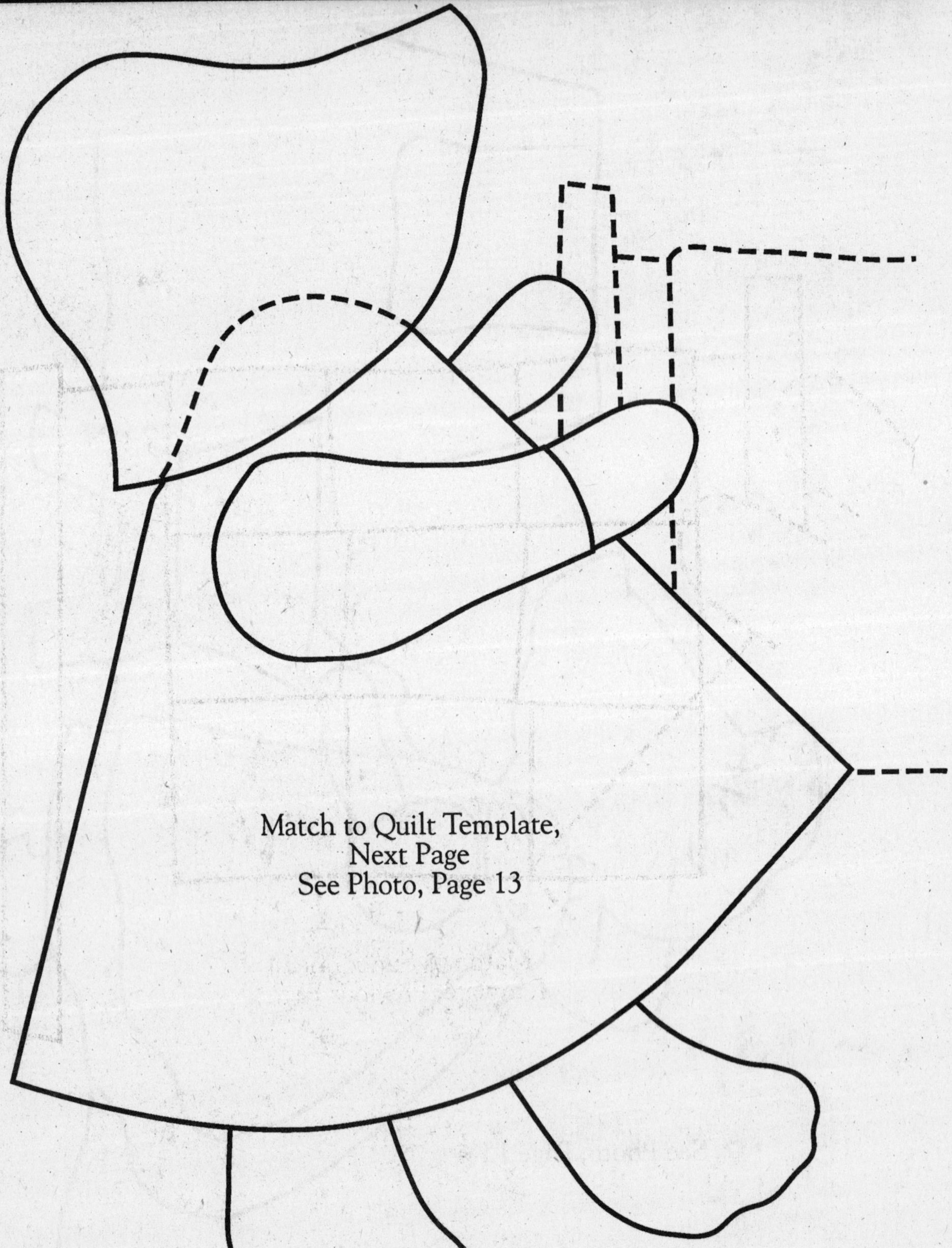

Match to Quilt Template,
Next Page
See Photo, Page 13

Sunbonnet
FAMILY REUNION

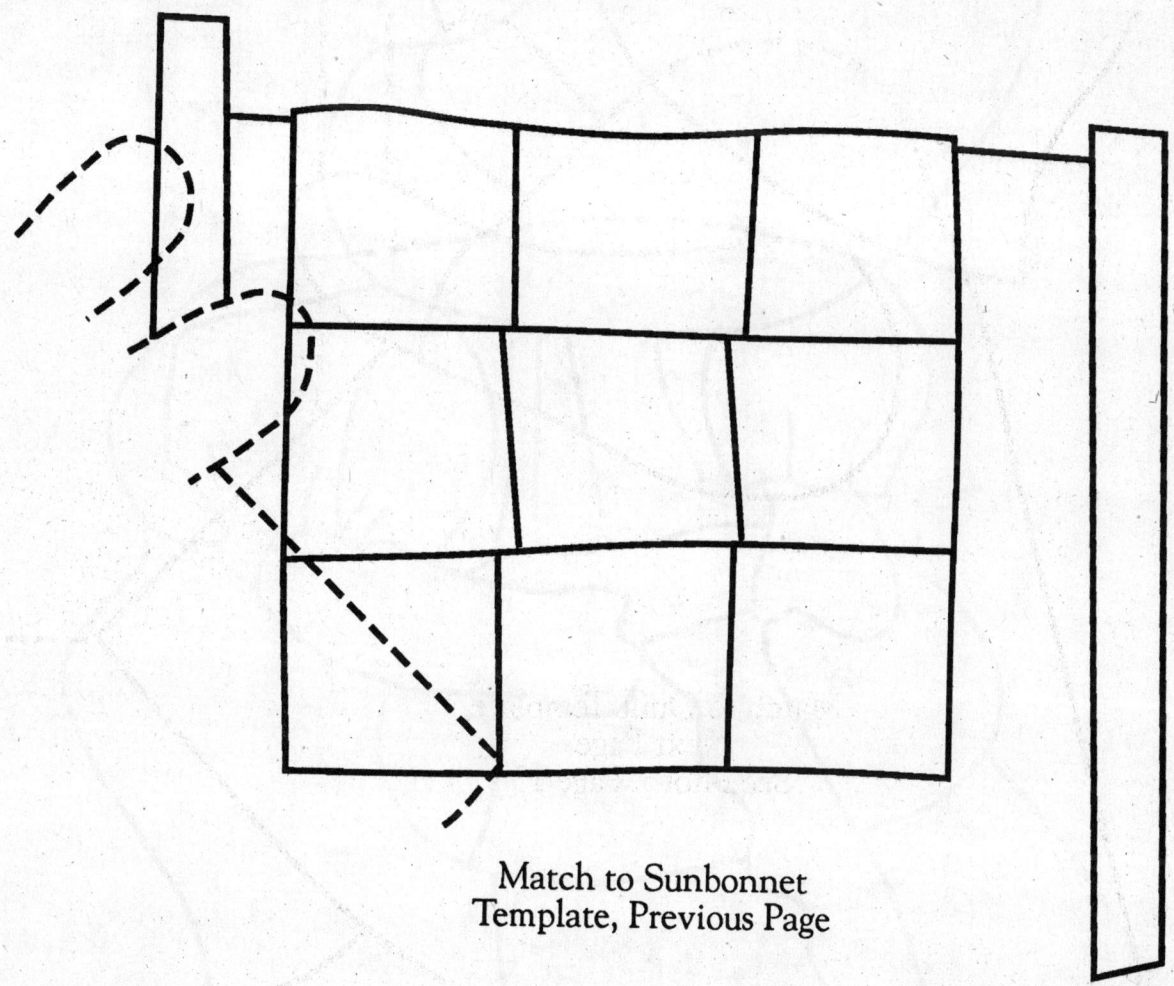

Match to Sunbonnet
Template, Previous Page

Sunbonnet FAMILY REUNION

The Lacemaker
Judy M. Sweets • Lawrence, KS

See Photo, Page 13

Quilting Sue
Lou Speed • Starkville, MS

See Photo, Page 13

Sunbonnet FAMILY REUNION

Suzanne
Bonnie White • Boyd, TX

See Photo, Page 14

1935 Sunbonnet
Louise Barney • Broadview Heights, OH

Adapted from *Kansas City Star*

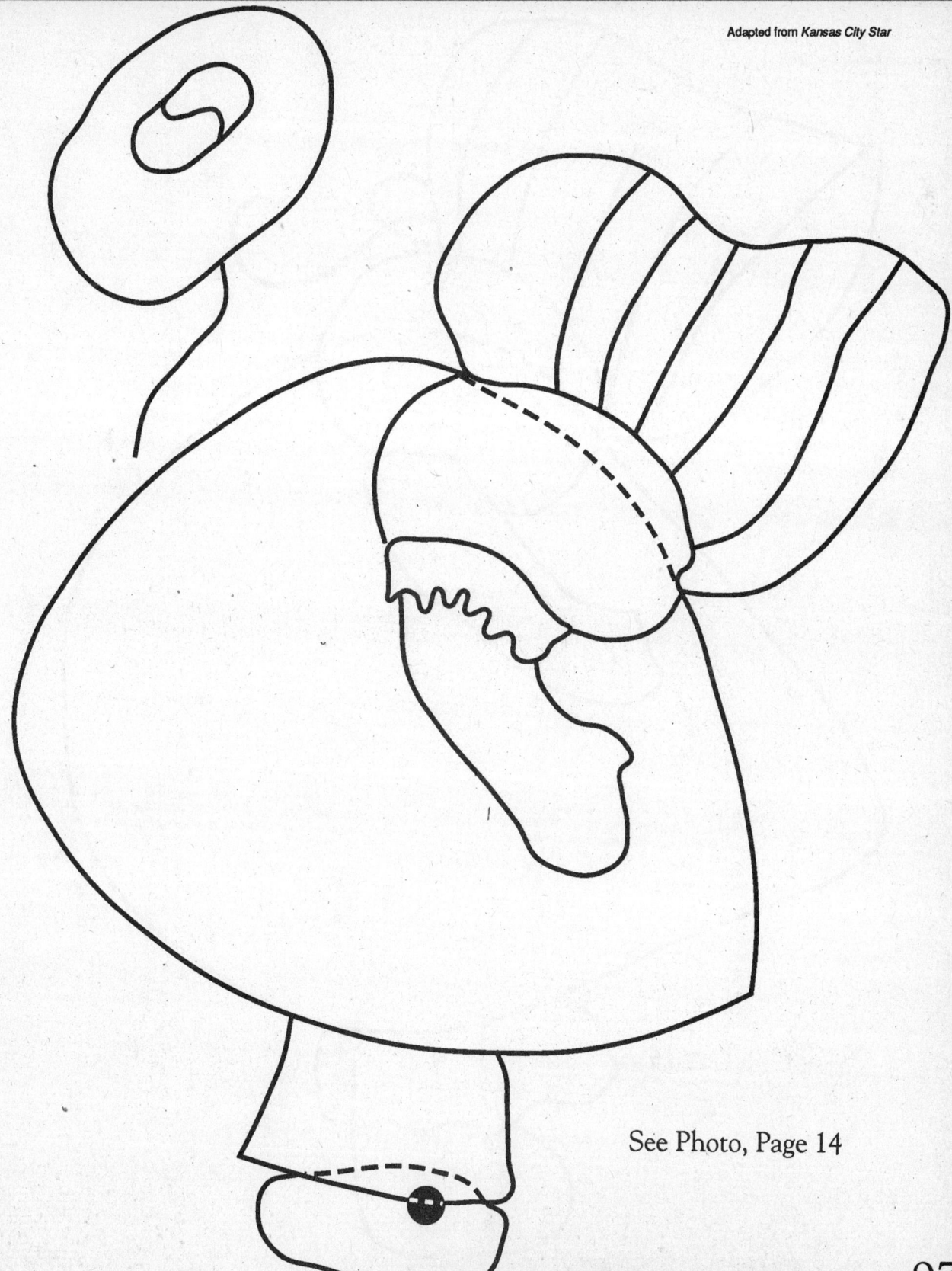

See Photo, Page 14

Here Comes Sunbonnet Sue
Theresa Filley • Leavenworth, KS

Adapted from *Kansas City Star*

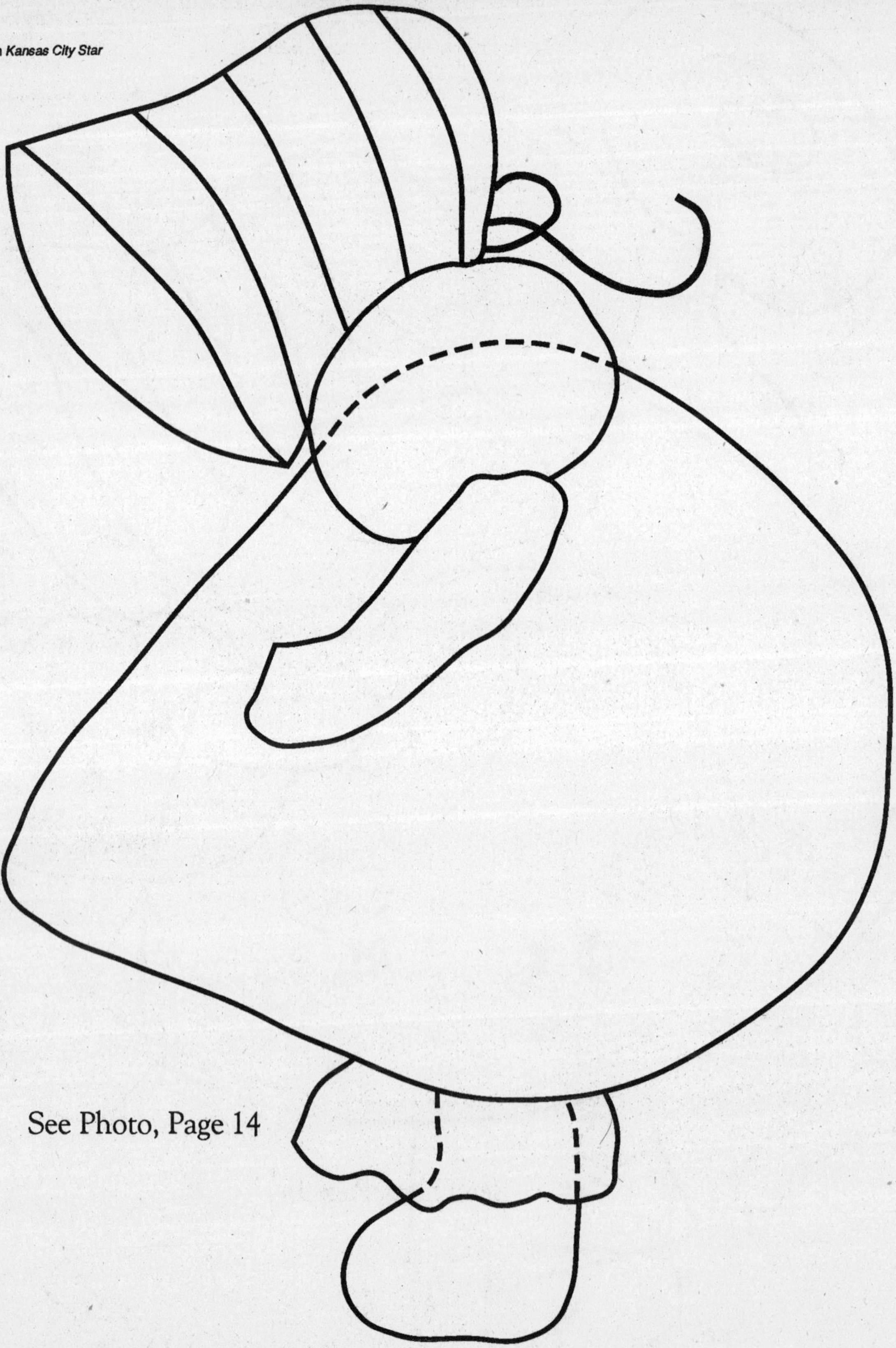

See Photo, Page 14

October Sue
Maryanne Cammarata • Summit, AR

Adapted from Edie Haynie

See Photo, Page 14

Sunbonnet Sue
Miriam Reed • Grandview, MO

Adapted from *Kansas City Star*

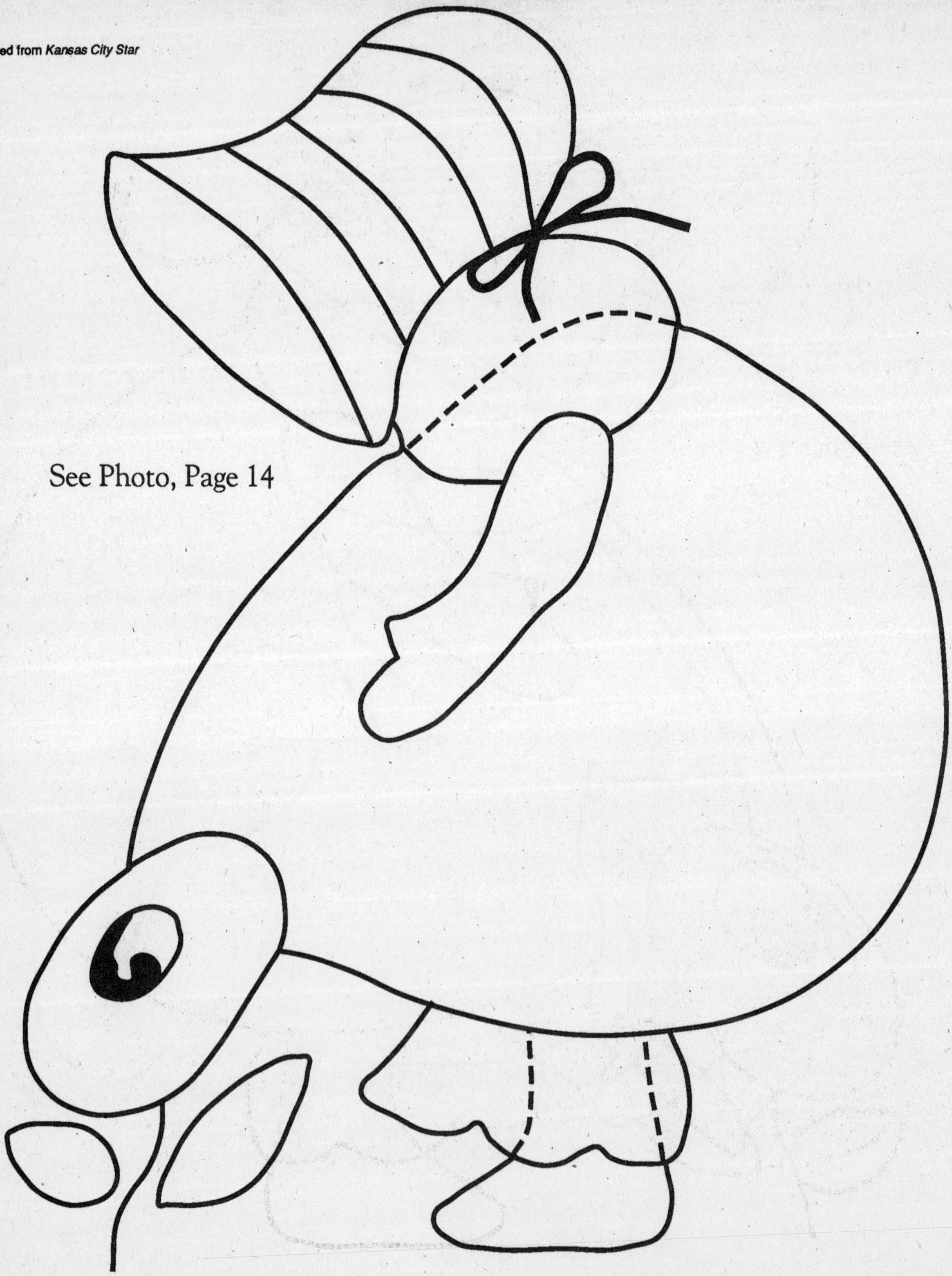

See Photo, Page 14

Kansas City's Sue
Margaret Youngberg • Chanute, KS

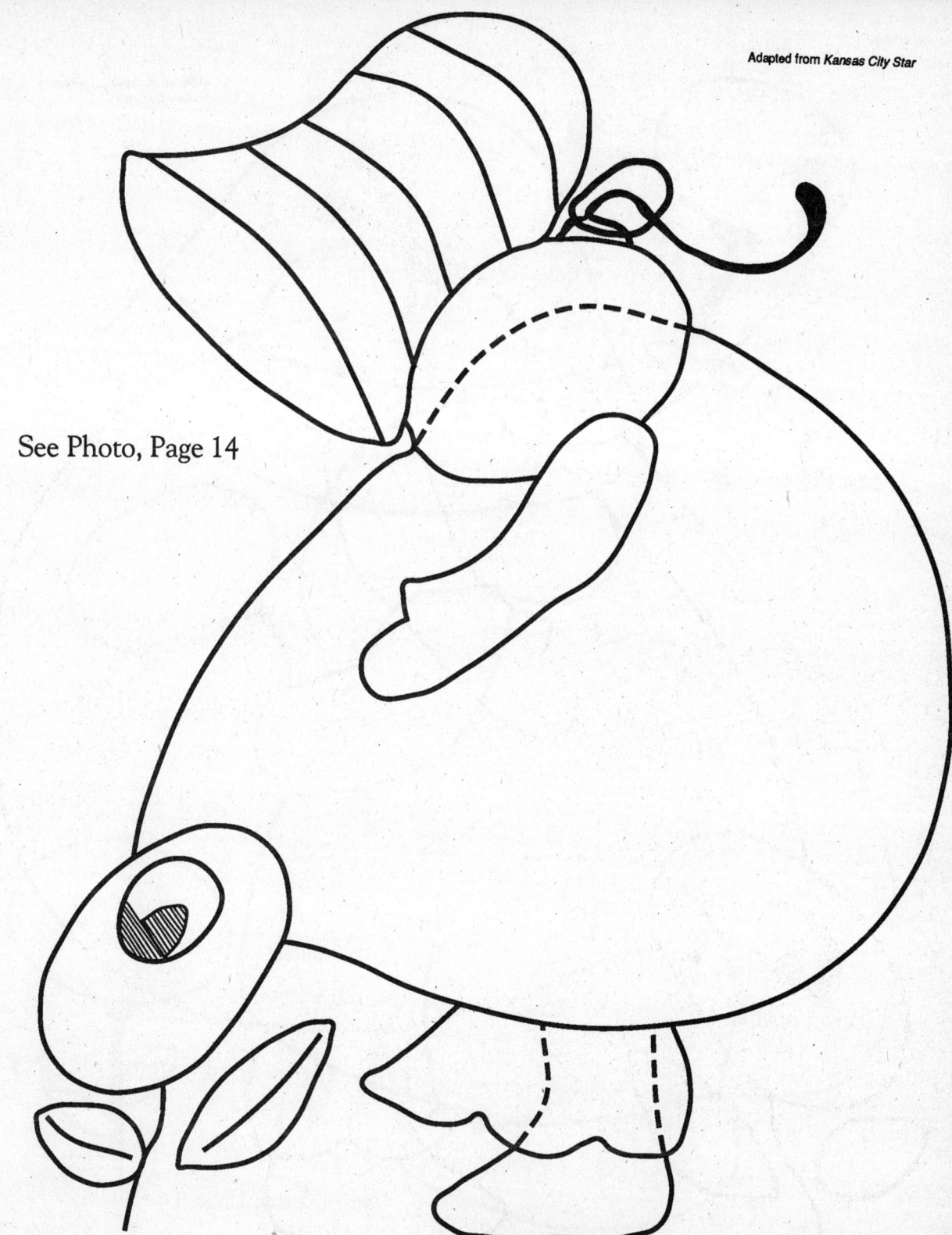

Adapted from *Kansas City Star*

See Photo, Page 14

Sunbonnet Family Reunion

Sunbonnet Sue
Gertrude M. Gerkey • Decatur, MI

Adapted from pattern printed in *Country Quilts*

See Photo, Page 14

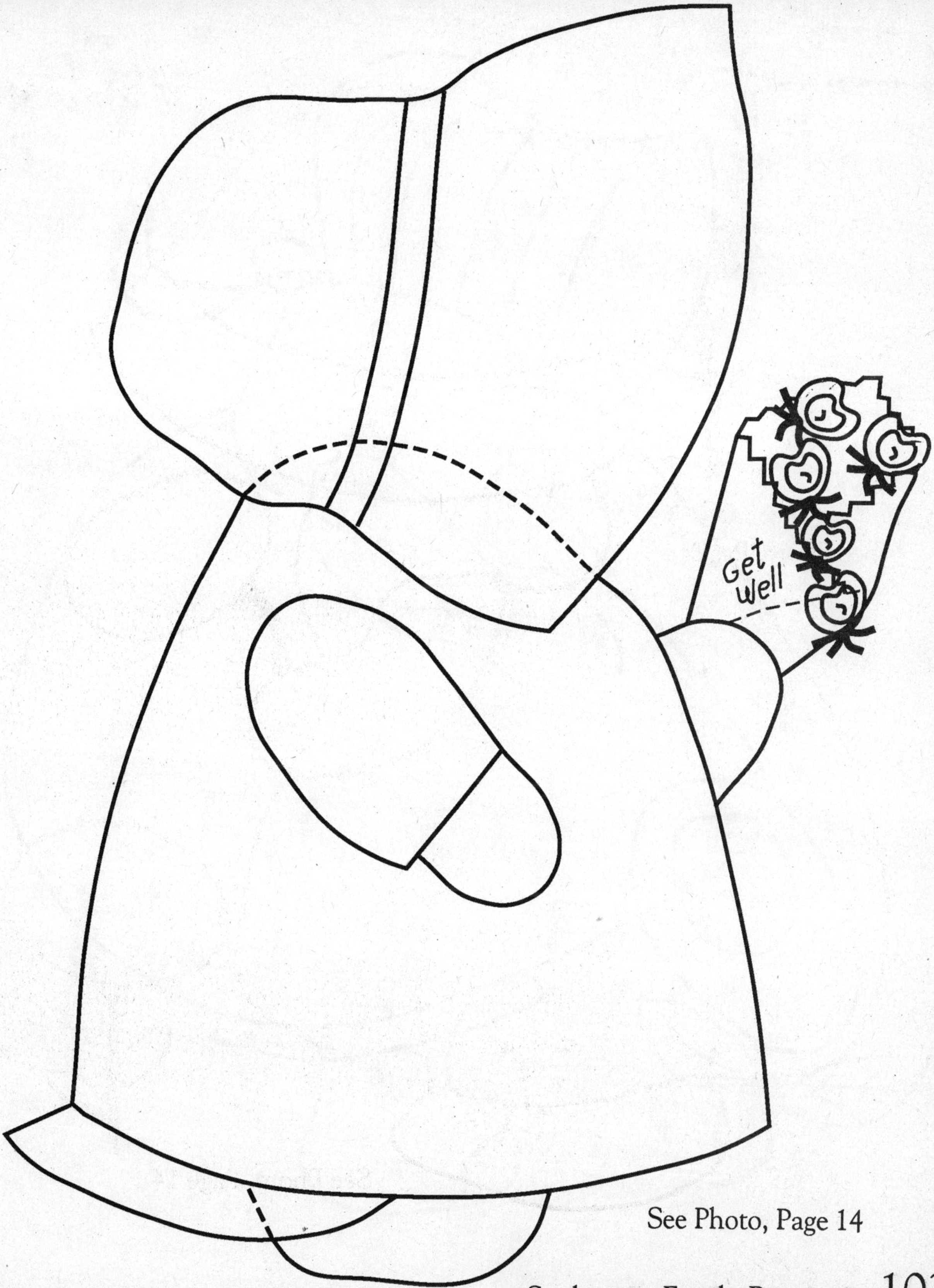

From My Garden, Dear Friend
Mary Ellen Frenzel • Oshkosh, WI

See Photo, Page 14

Sunbonnet Sue
Esther Stone • Davis City, IA

Adapted from *Kansas City Star*

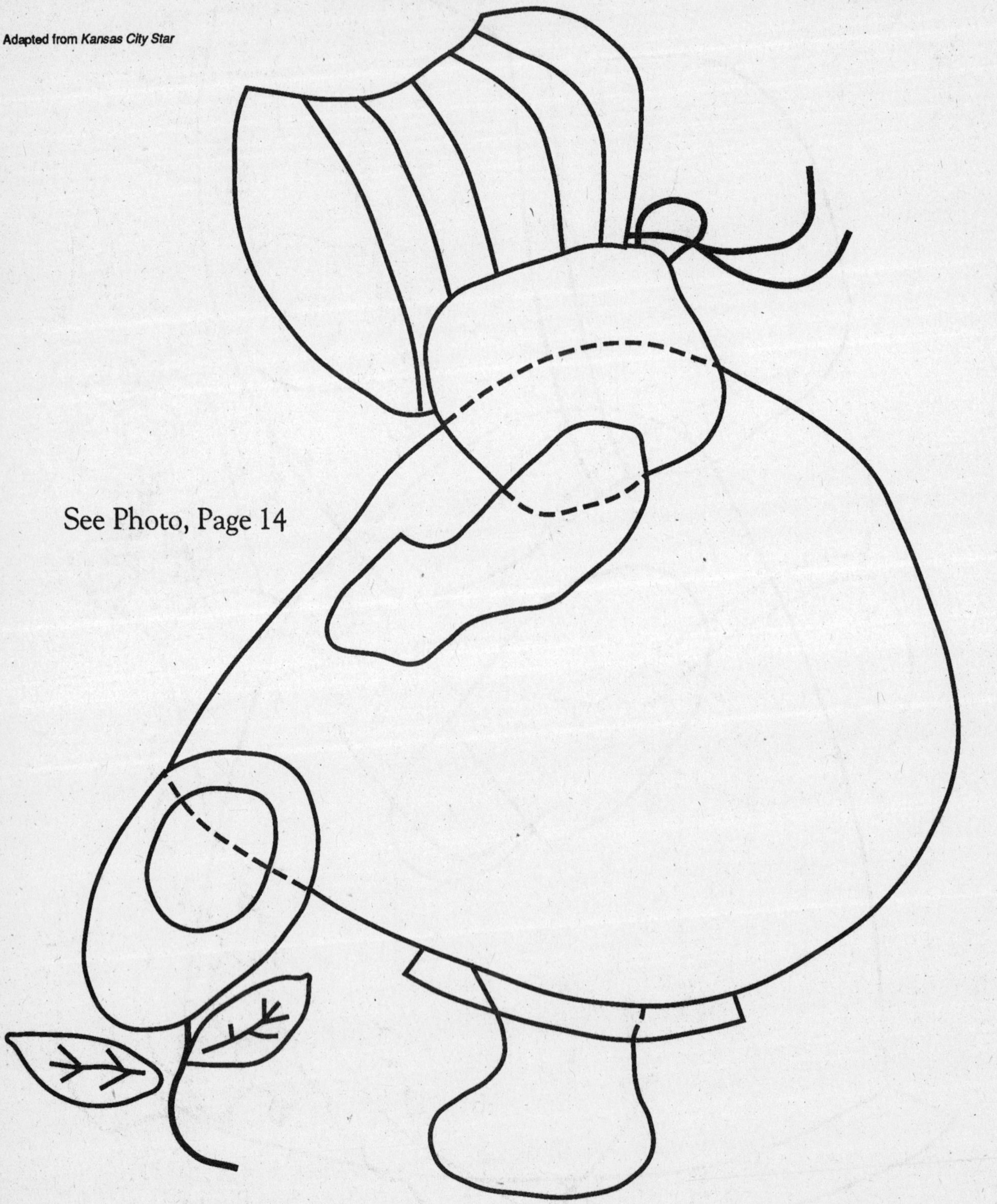

See Photo, Page 14

Flower Garden
Janet Smith • Gonzales, TX

See Photo, Page 15

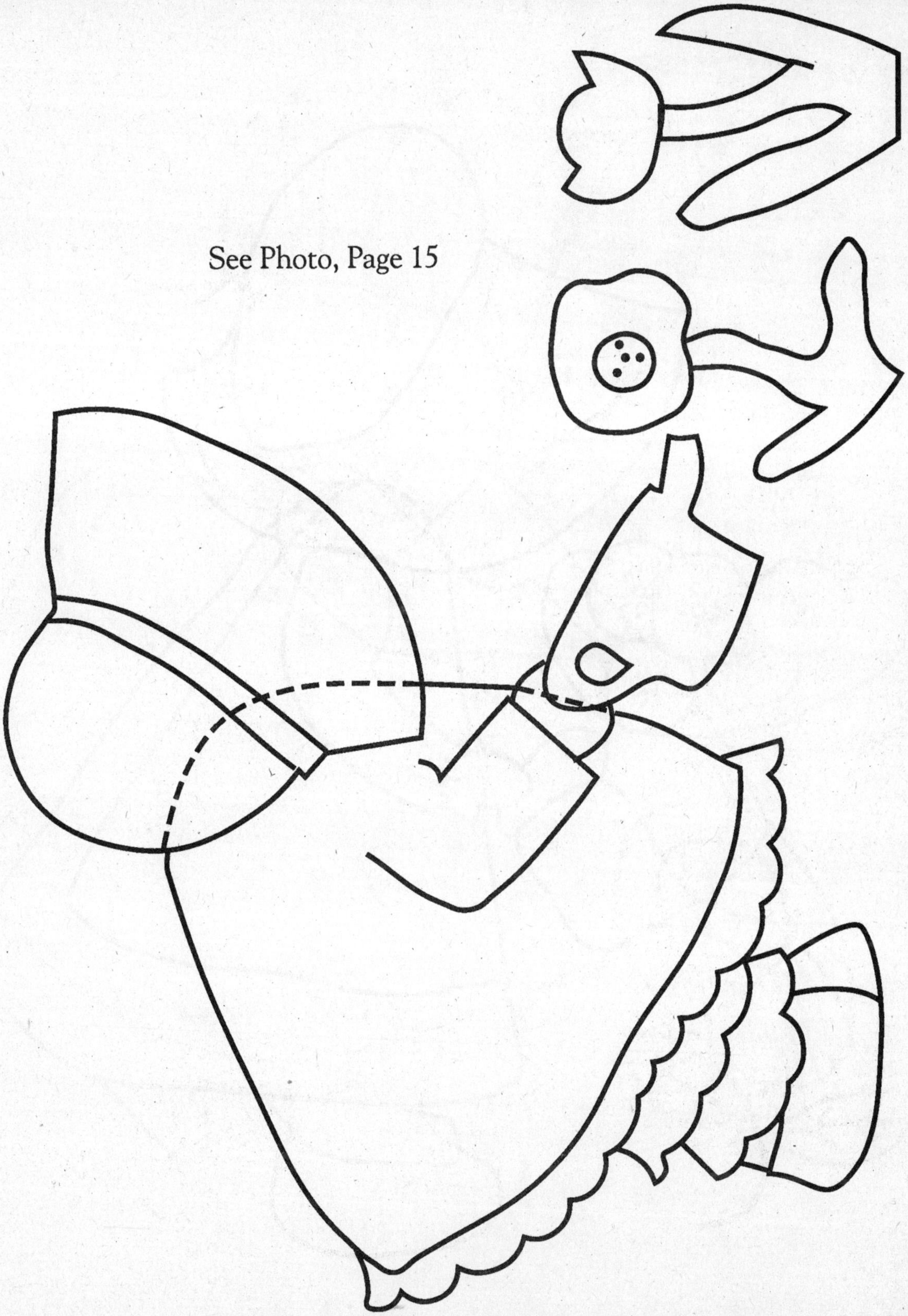

Sunbonnet FAMILY REUNION

Help Your Garden Grow
Ann Jensen • Richland, WA

See Photo, Page 15

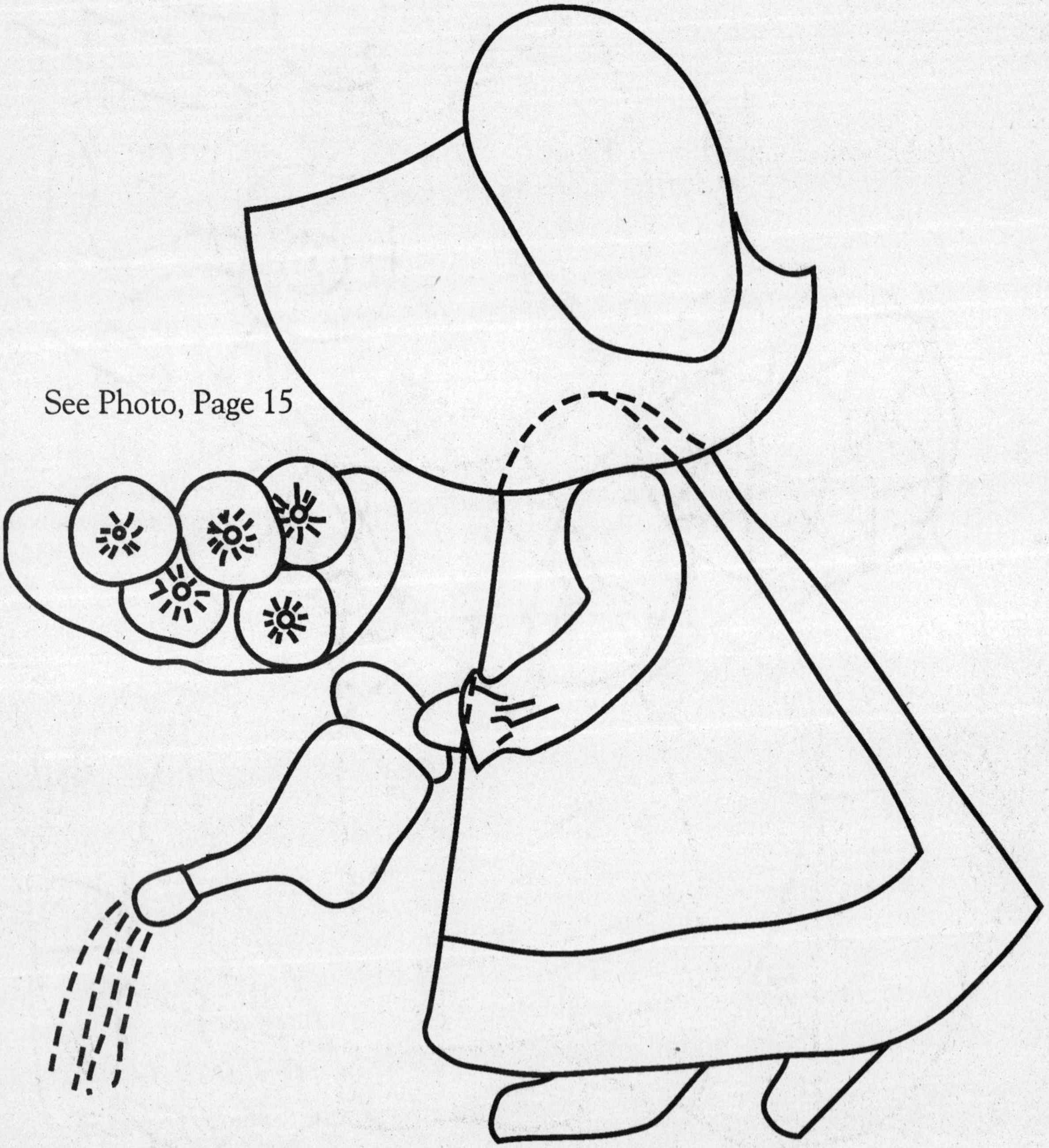

Kansas Baby
Margaret Bender • Danville, CA

See Photo, Page 15

Adapted from *Quilt Kansas* by Jean Mitchell

Sunflower Sue
Norma I. Abbott • Gardner, KS

See Photo, Page 15

Ring Around The Posie
Ann S. Huffman • Choctaw, OK

See Photo, Page 15

Sunbonnet FAMILY REUNION

Canada's Sunflower Sue
Dorothy Reif • Windsor, Ont., Canada

See Photo, Page 15

110 Sunbonnet Family Reunion

Love
Rita J. Blake • Baldwin, PA

See Photo, Page 15

Sunbonnet Family Reunion

Working & Playing With Love
Debby Bingham • Baytown, TX

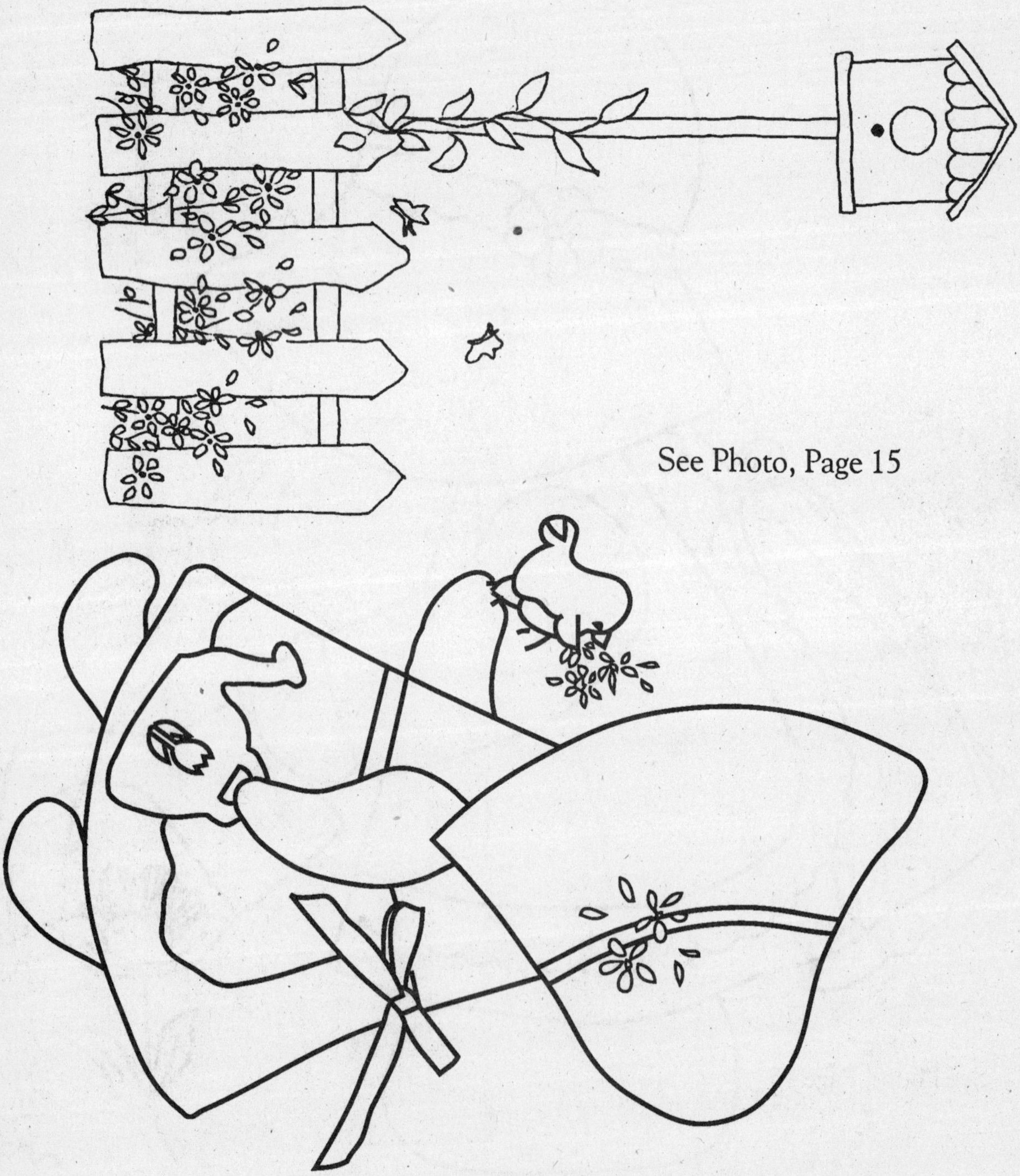

See Photo, Page 15

All Dressed Up
June Wolpert • Nashville, IN

See Photo, Page 15

Sunbonnet Family Reunion

Books & Butterflies
Mariah Wilson • Gonzales, TX

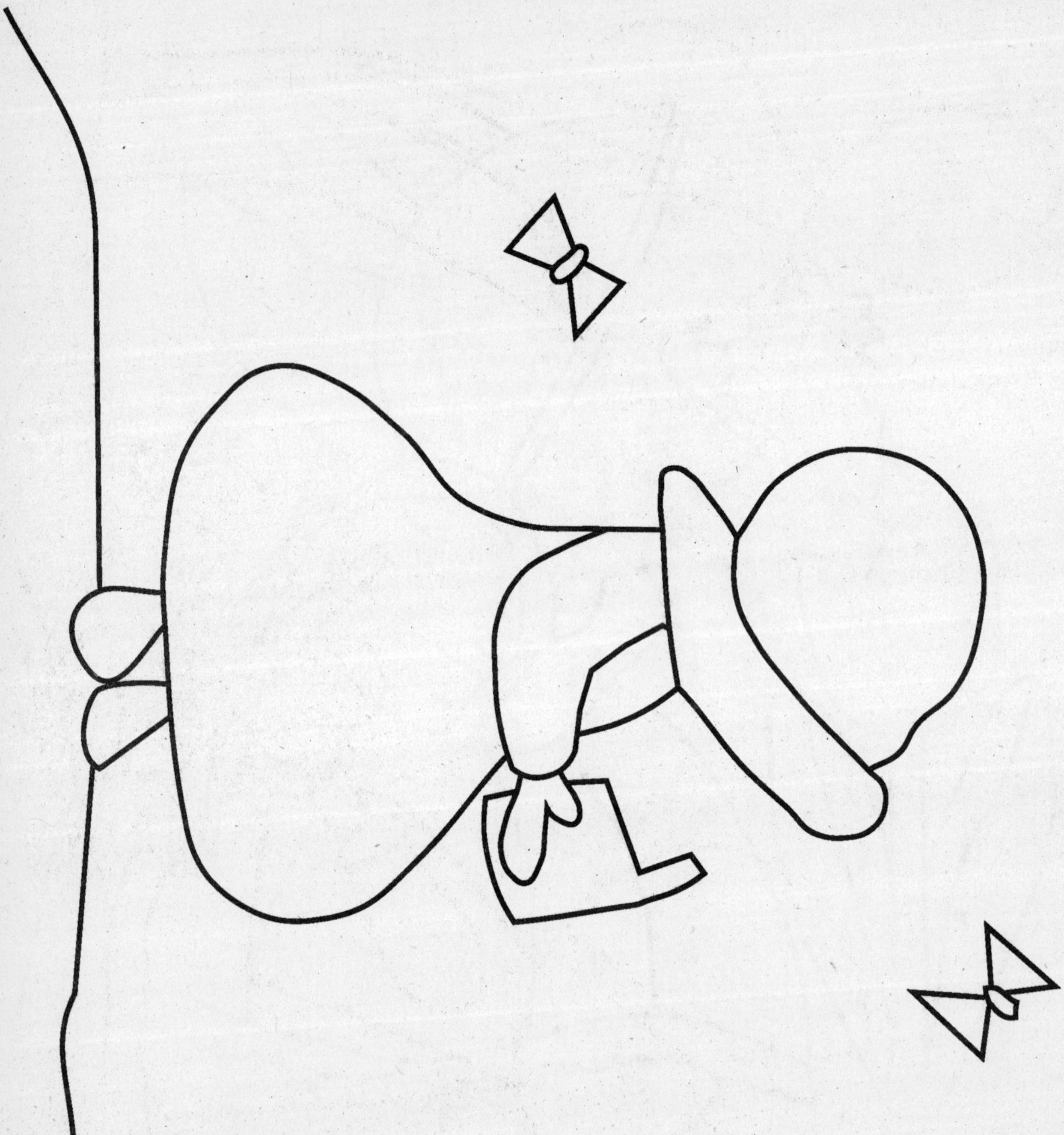

See Photo, Page 16

Sue's Iris, Texas Style
Eleanor Bain • Carlinville, IL

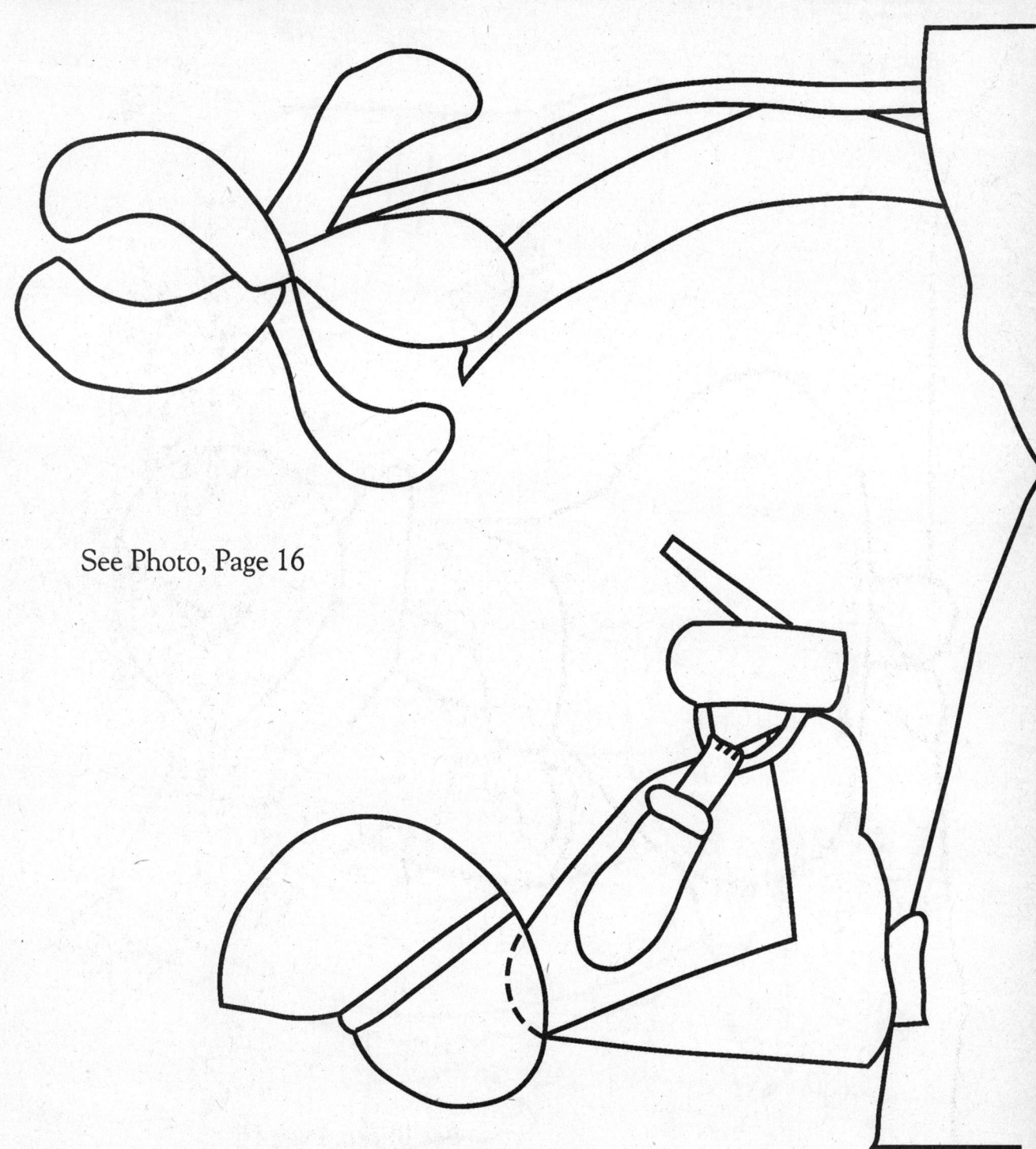

See Photo, Page 16

Sunbonnet Sue With Her Flowers
Carol Welch • Pleasant Plains, IL

Adapted from *A Meet of the Sunbonnet Children* by Betty Hagerman

See Photo, Page 16

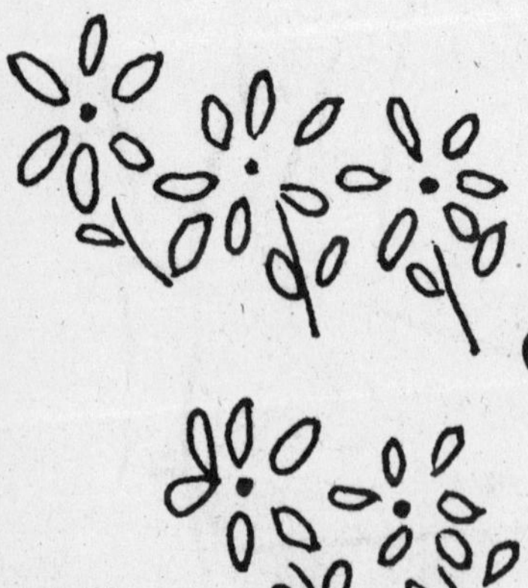

Sunbonnet Sarah
Colleen Hall • Overland Park, KS

See Photo, Page 16

Sunbonnet FAMILY REUNION

Picking Magentas
Lavona Keltner • Camdenton, MO

Adapted from a pattern printed in a *Quilter's Newsletter Magazine*

Piece Templates

Cut squares and triangles as shown. Cut two borders of Light Print 1, 1-1/2" x 12-1/2". Cut two borders of Light Print 1, 1-1/2" x 11-1/2". Use guide below for piecing. Refer to photo, page 16 for color possibilities.

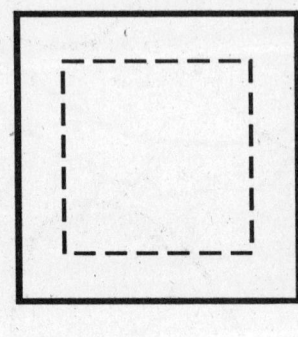
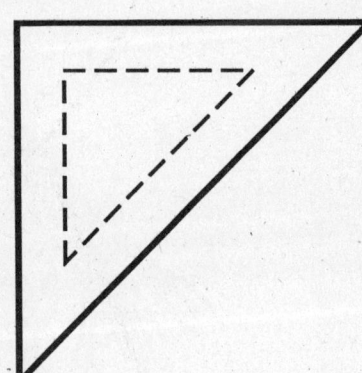

Light Print 1
34 Squares
31 Triangles

Dark Print 1
23 Squares
18 Triangles

Light Print 2
3 Squares
11 Triangles

Dark Print 2
10 Triangles

Solid
4 Squares
15 Triangles

Dark Print 3
2 Squares

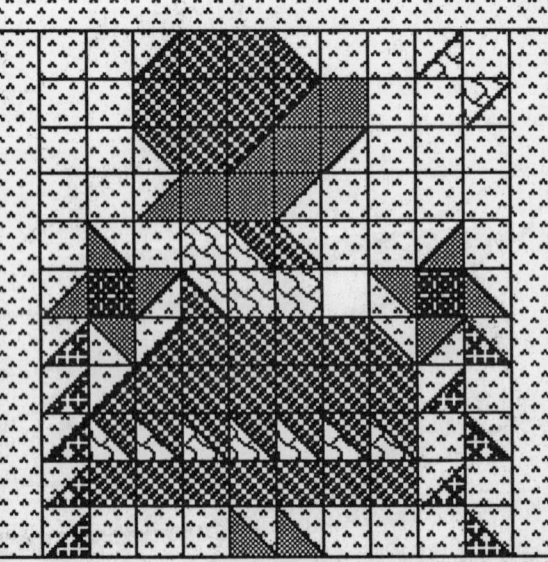

Sunbonnet Sunday Best
Mary Gish • Michigan City, IN

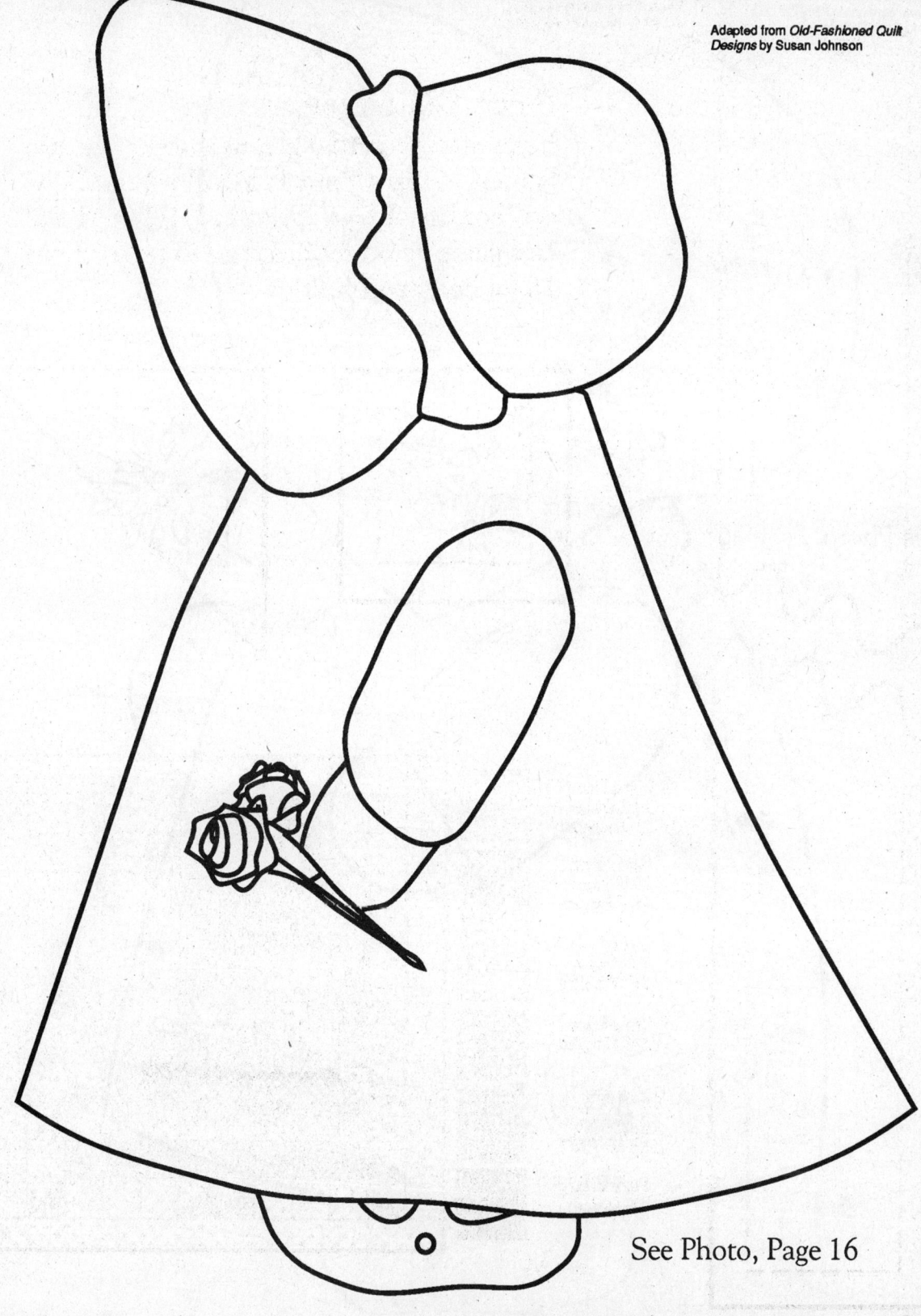

Adapted from *Old-Fashioned Quilt Designs* by Susan Johnson

See Photo, Page 16

Sunbonnet FAMILY REUNION

Traditional Sunbonnet Sue-1920s
Wilma Crawford • Brainerd, MN

Adapted from *Sunbonnet Family of Quilt Patterns* by Delores Hinson

See Photo, Page 16

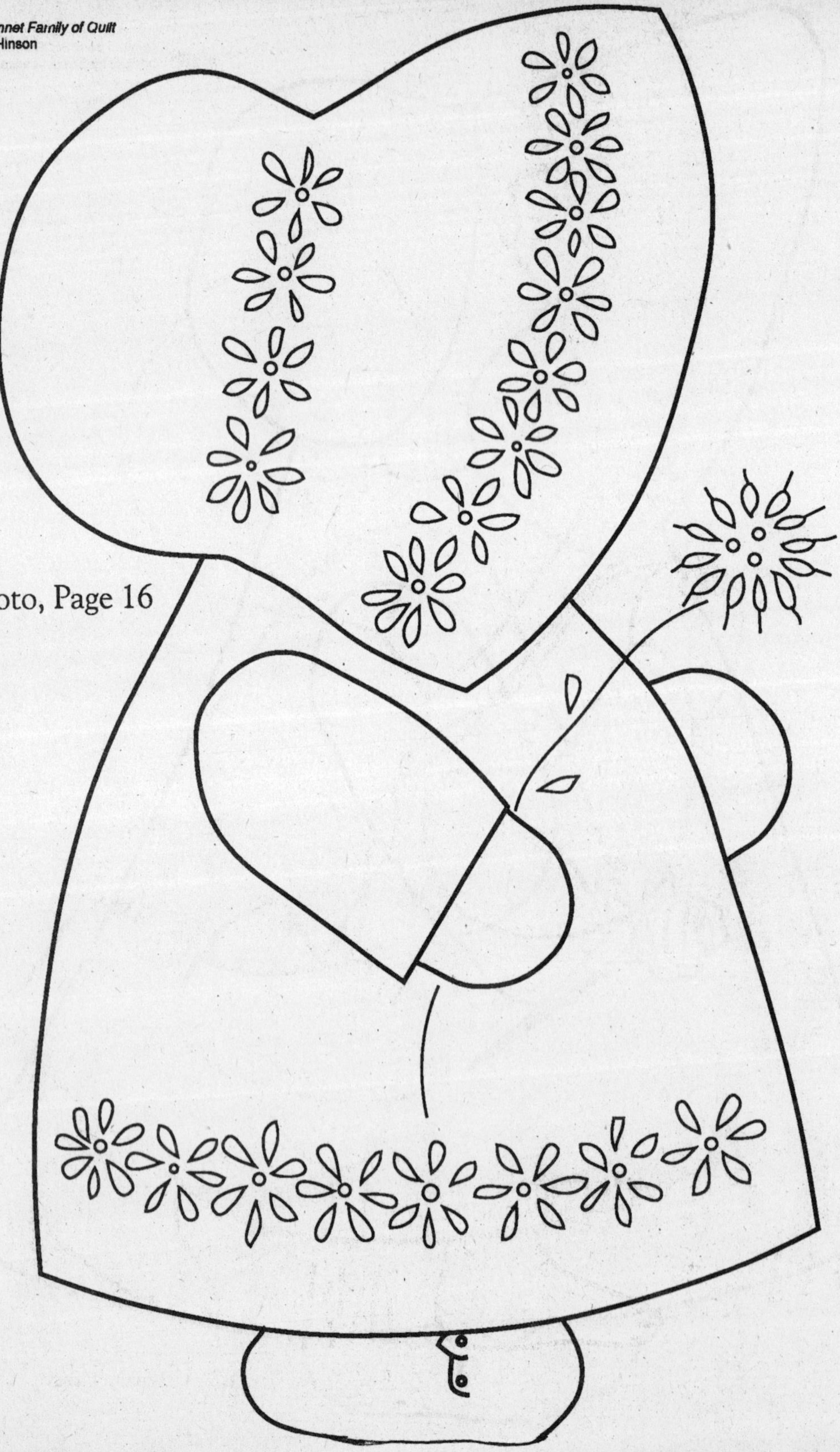

A Romp In The Grass
Catherine R. Jones • Fairbanks, AK

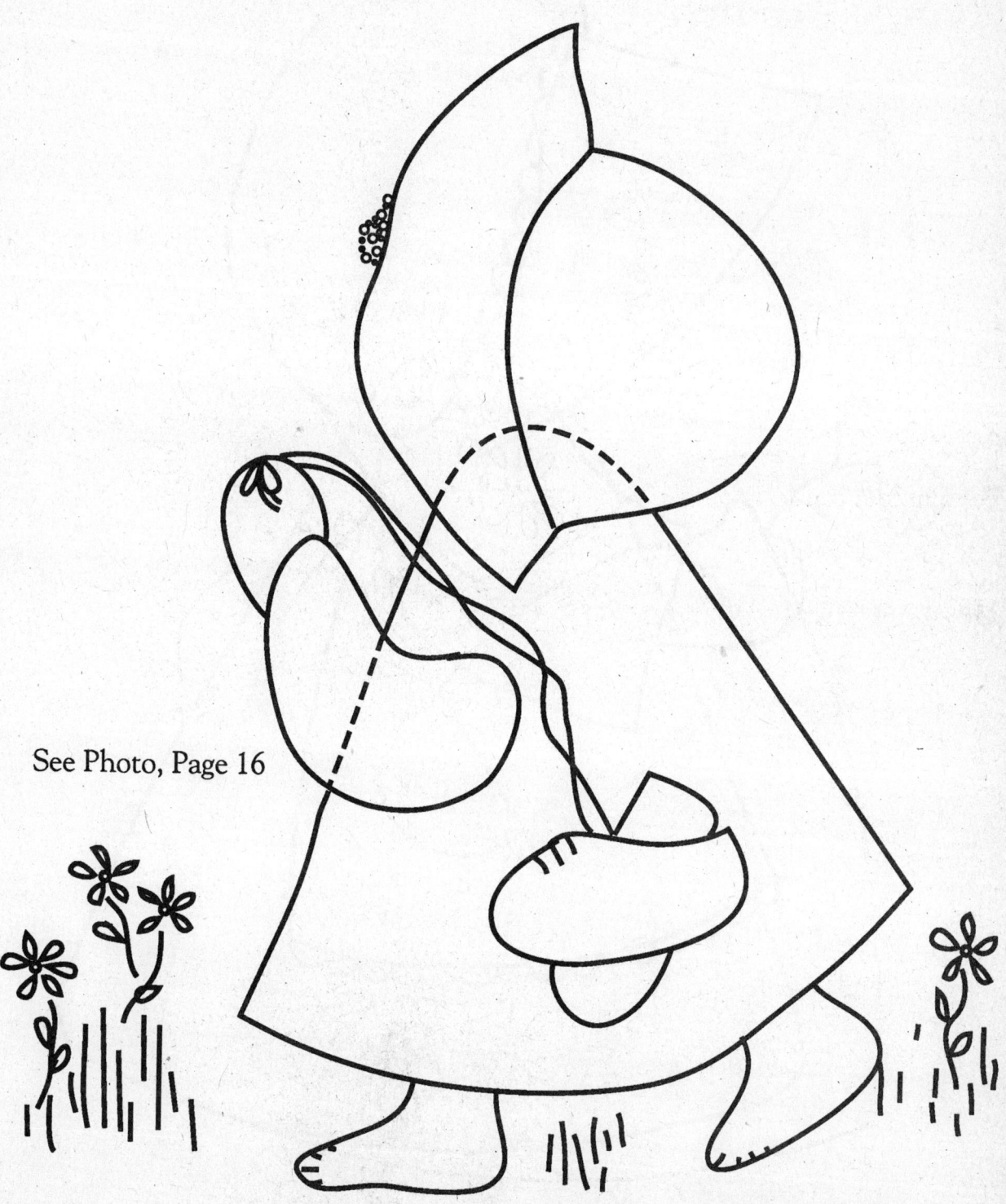

See Photo, Page 16

Sunbonnet FAMILY REUNION

Spring Bonnet Sue
Marge Eakins • La Puente, CA

See Photo, Page 16

Strolling Sue
Mildred Kitchens • Kennean City, FL

See Photo, Page 17

Sunbonnet Sue
Vicki Olson • Wyoming, MN

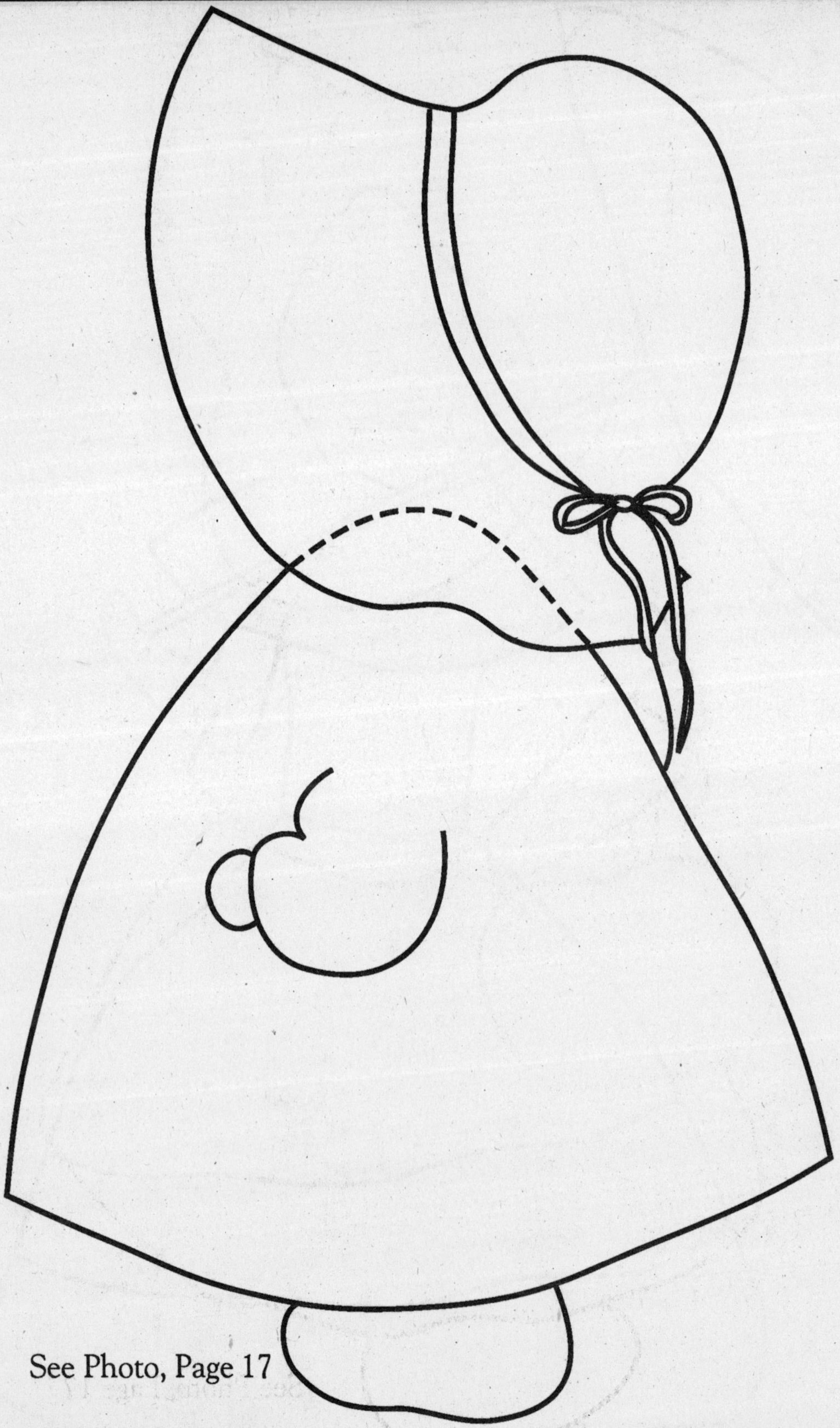

See Photo, Page 17

Going Shopping
Louise H. Stenstrom • Sanford, FL

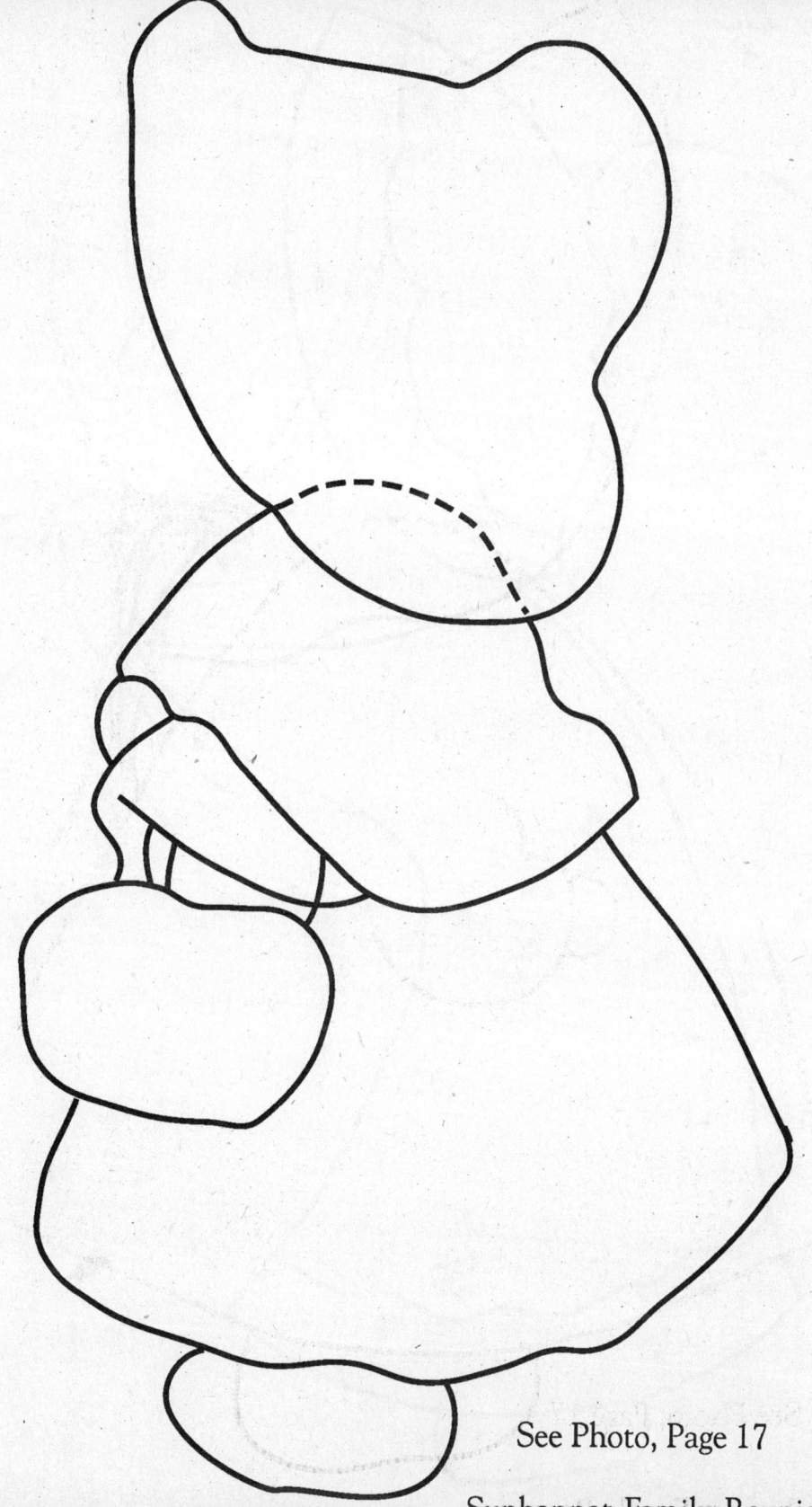

See Photo, Page 17

Little Sunbonnet
Kate Mitchell • Anderson, IN

Adapted from *Sunbonnet Family of Quilt Patterns* by Delores Hinson

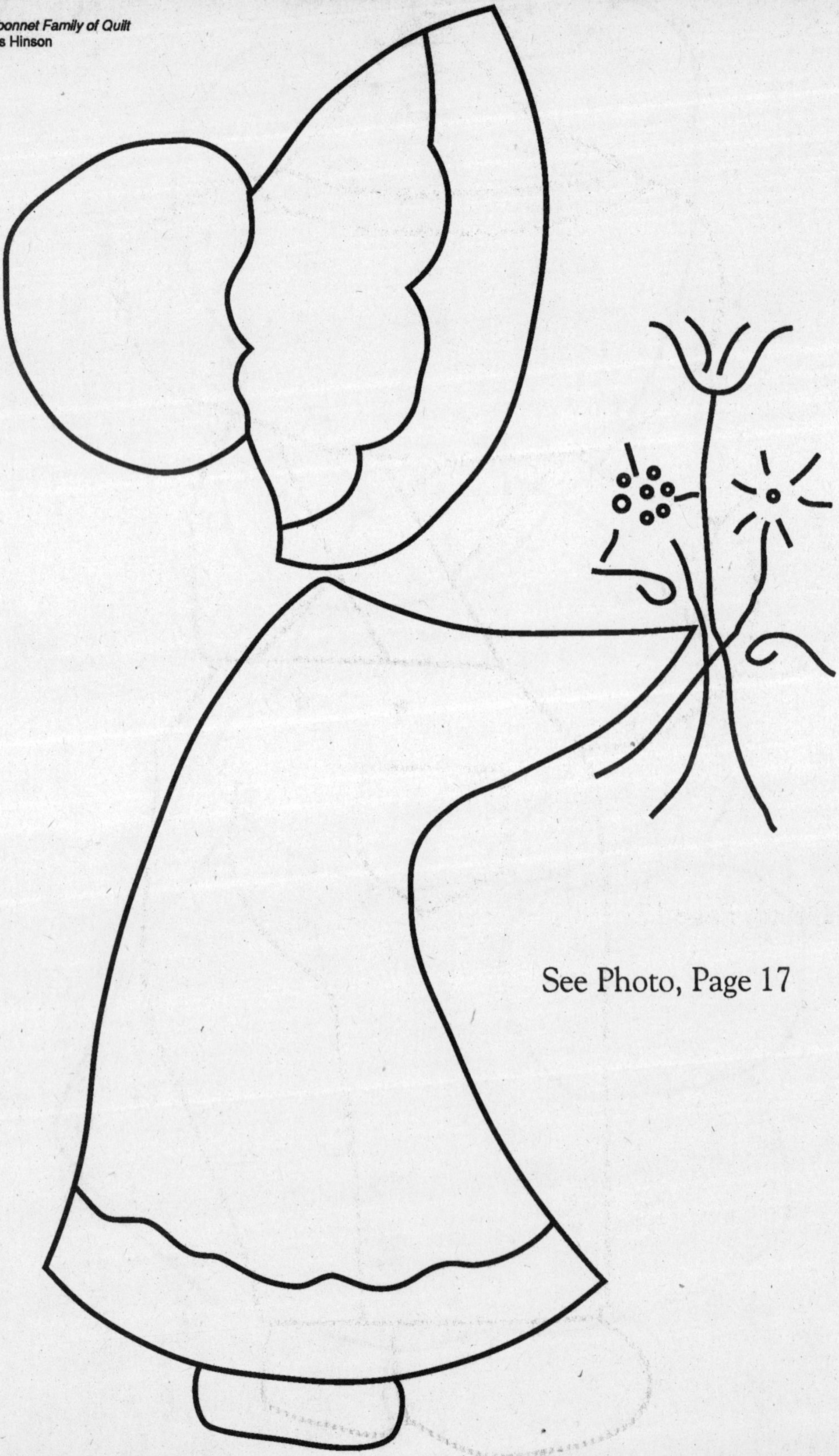

See Photo, Page 17

Overall Bill
Louise H. Stenstrom • Sanford, FL

Adapted from *Calico Hill Farms Pattern*

See Photo, Page 17

Sunbonnet Sue
Pauline Petty • Nashville, TN

See Photo, Page 17

Flowering Lady
Betty L. Purkey • Irvine, CA

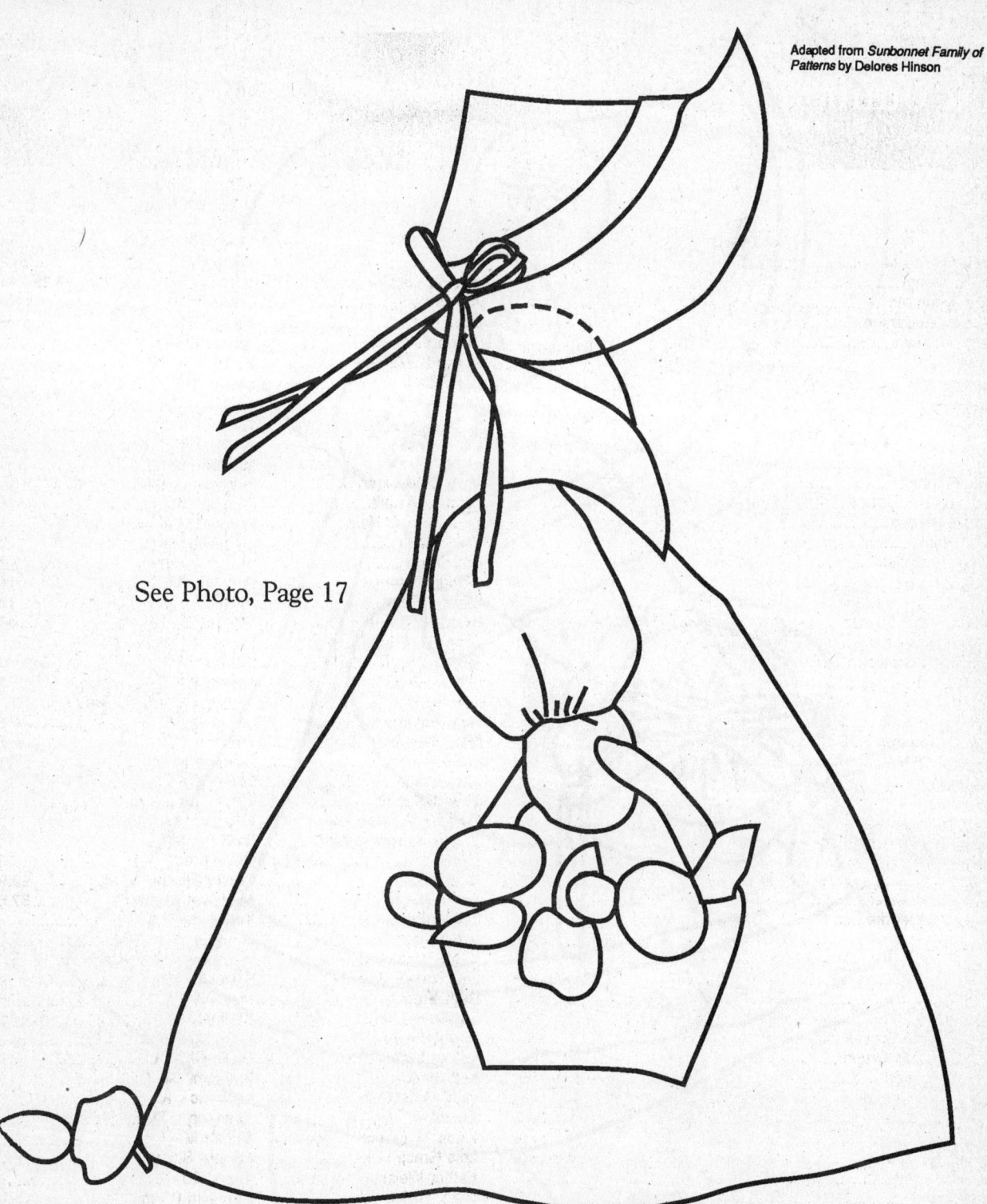

Adapted from *Sunbonnet Family of Patterns* by Delores Hinson

See Photo, Page 17

Sunbonnet Family Reunion

Sunbonnet Susie Yo-Yo
Mary Self • Gallion, AL

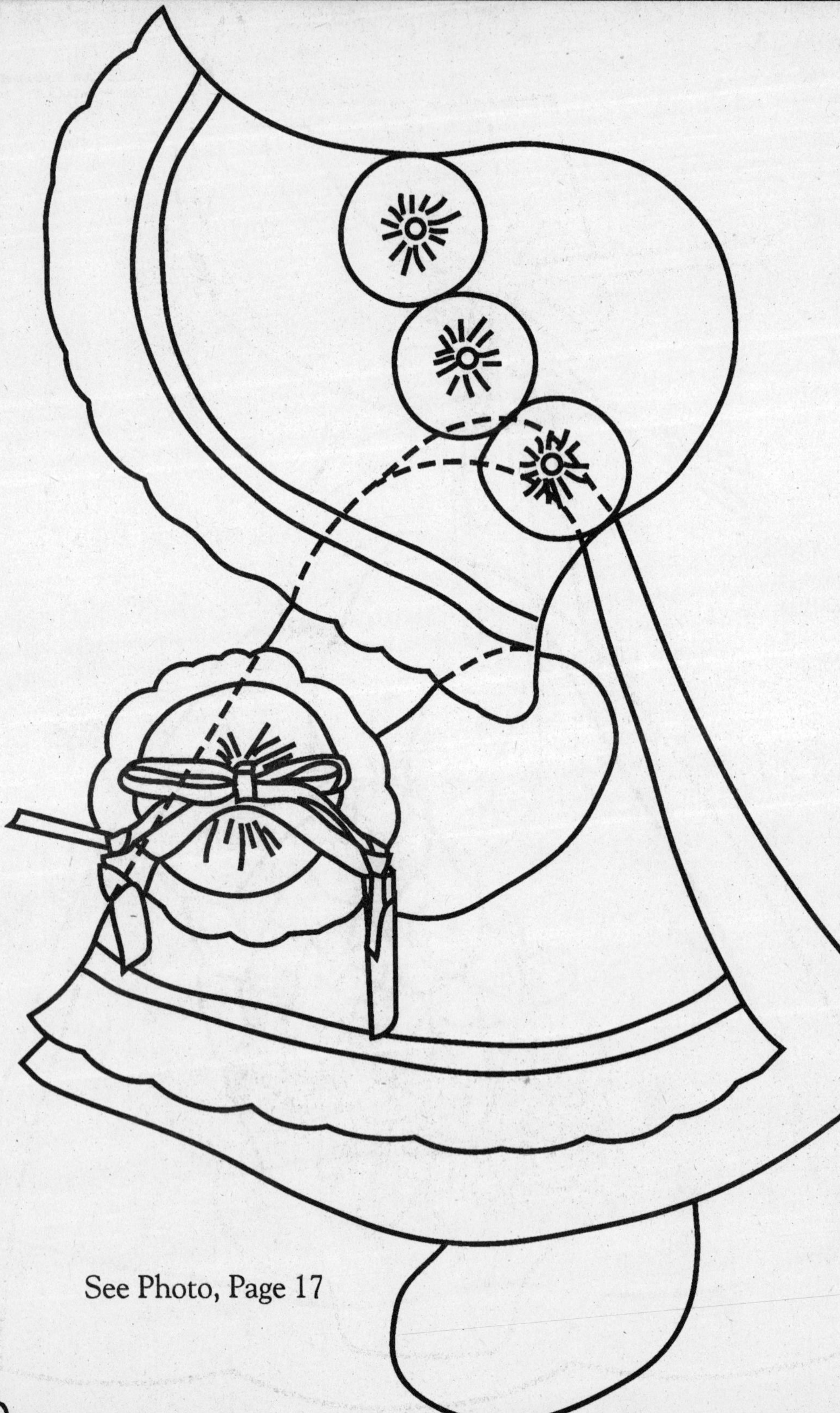

See Photo, Page 17

Colonial Flower Girl
Shari Schmidt • Turpin, OK

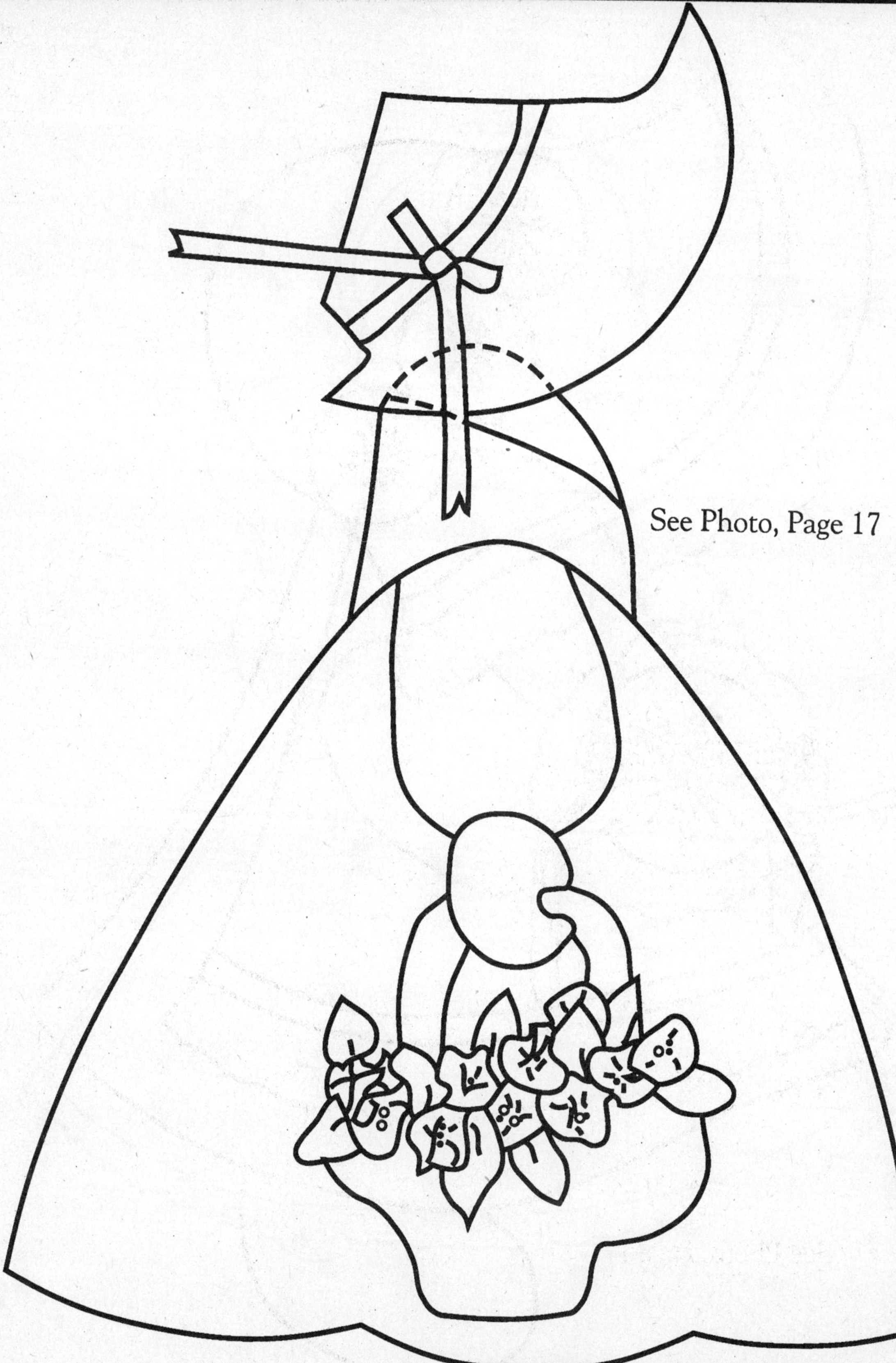

See Photo, Page 17

Sunbonnet FAMILY REUNION

Angel
Lois Grace Voigt • Bonner Springs, KS

See Photo, Page 18

Going To Church
Annadell Teems • Granbury, TX

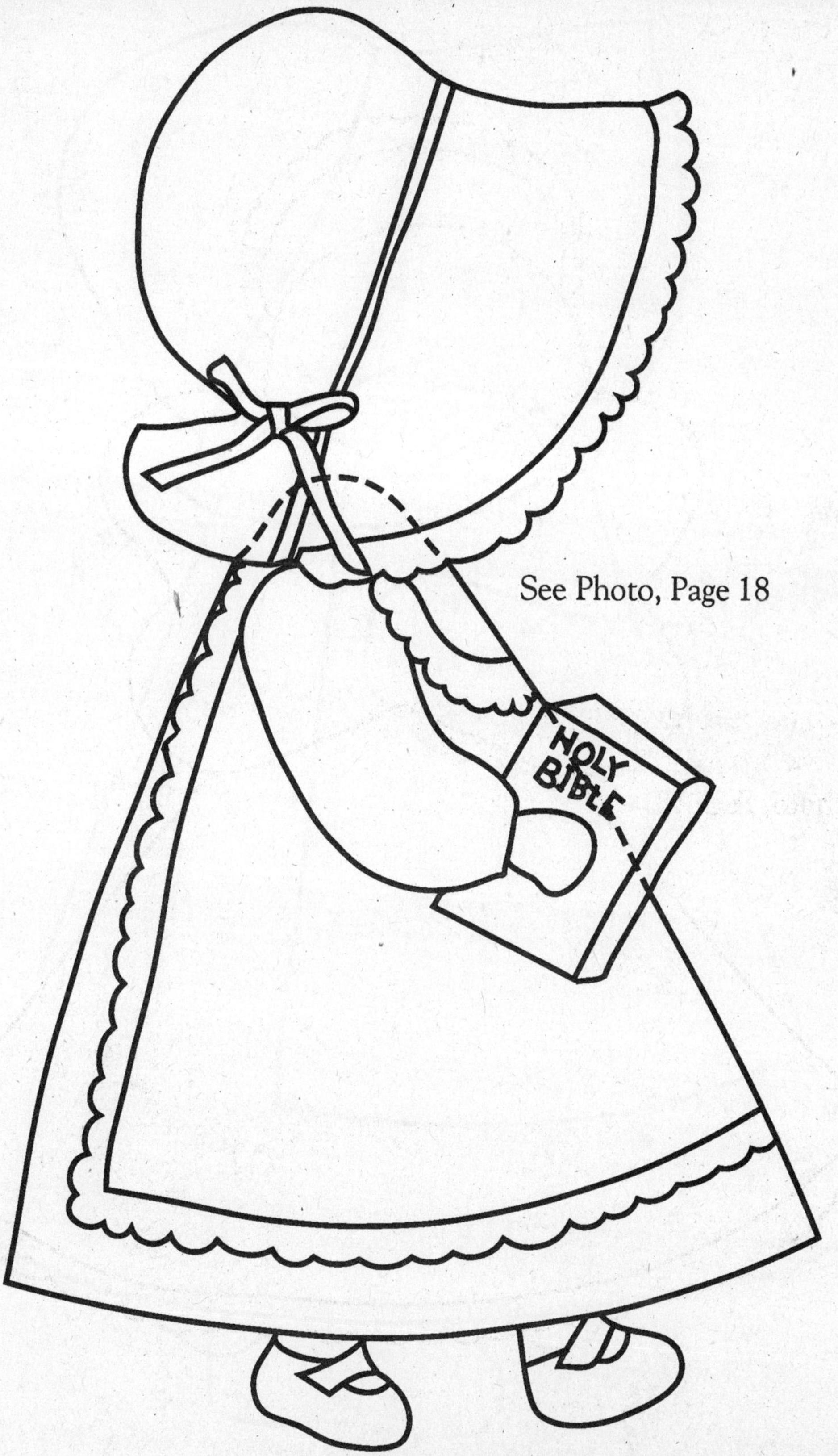

See Photo, Page 18

Calico Sue With Flowers
Phyllis Long • Lindsey, OH

See Photo, Page 18

Sunbonnet Saying Psalms
Mary Lu Beemer-Schofield • Lenox, IA

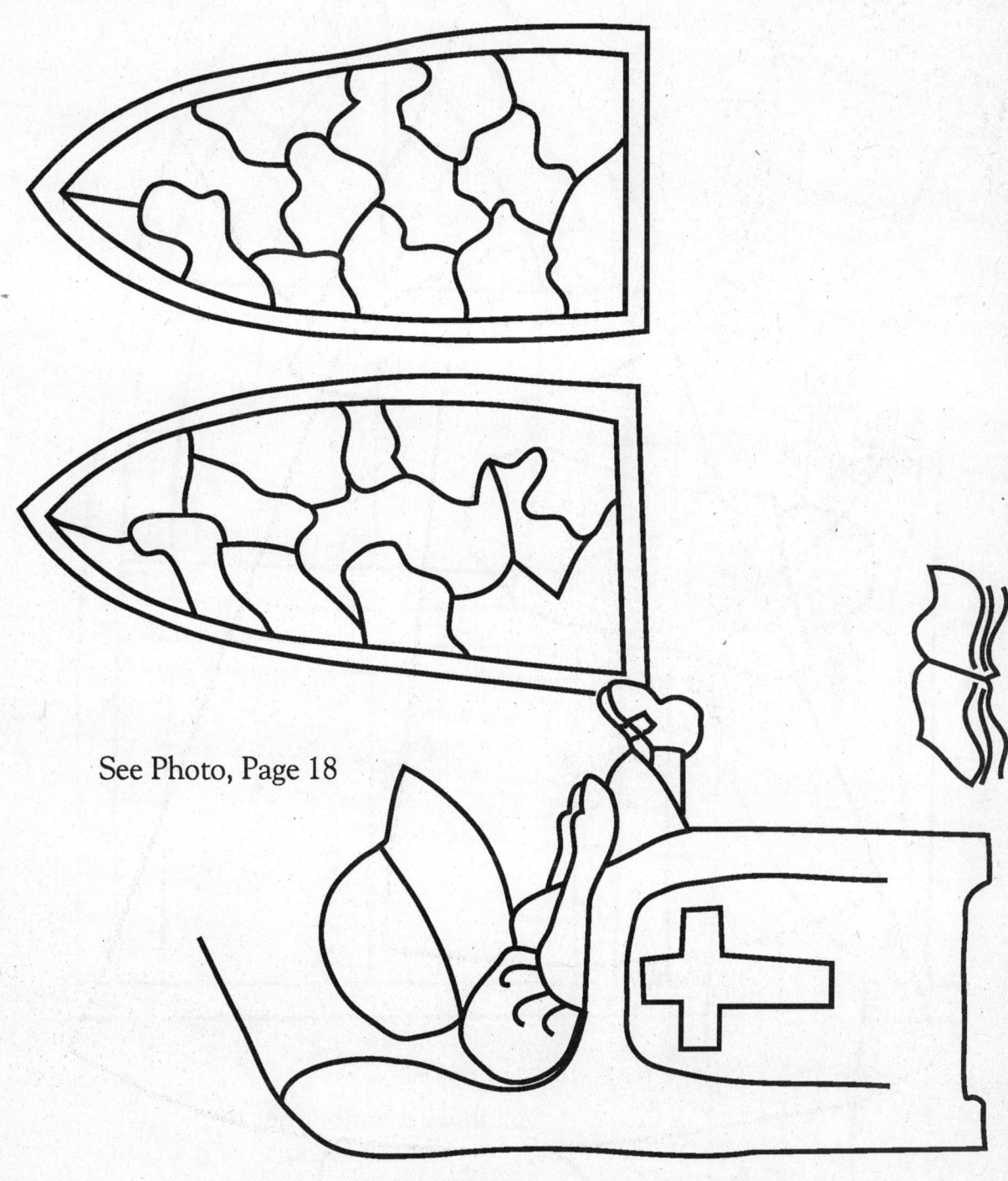

See Photo, Page 18

Sunbonnet FAMILY REUNION

Bill & Sue's Wedding
Susan Jean Faber • Dyer, IN

Match with Sunbonnet Bride,
Next Page
See Photo, Page 18

Match with Sunbonnet Groom, Previous Page
See Photo, Page 18

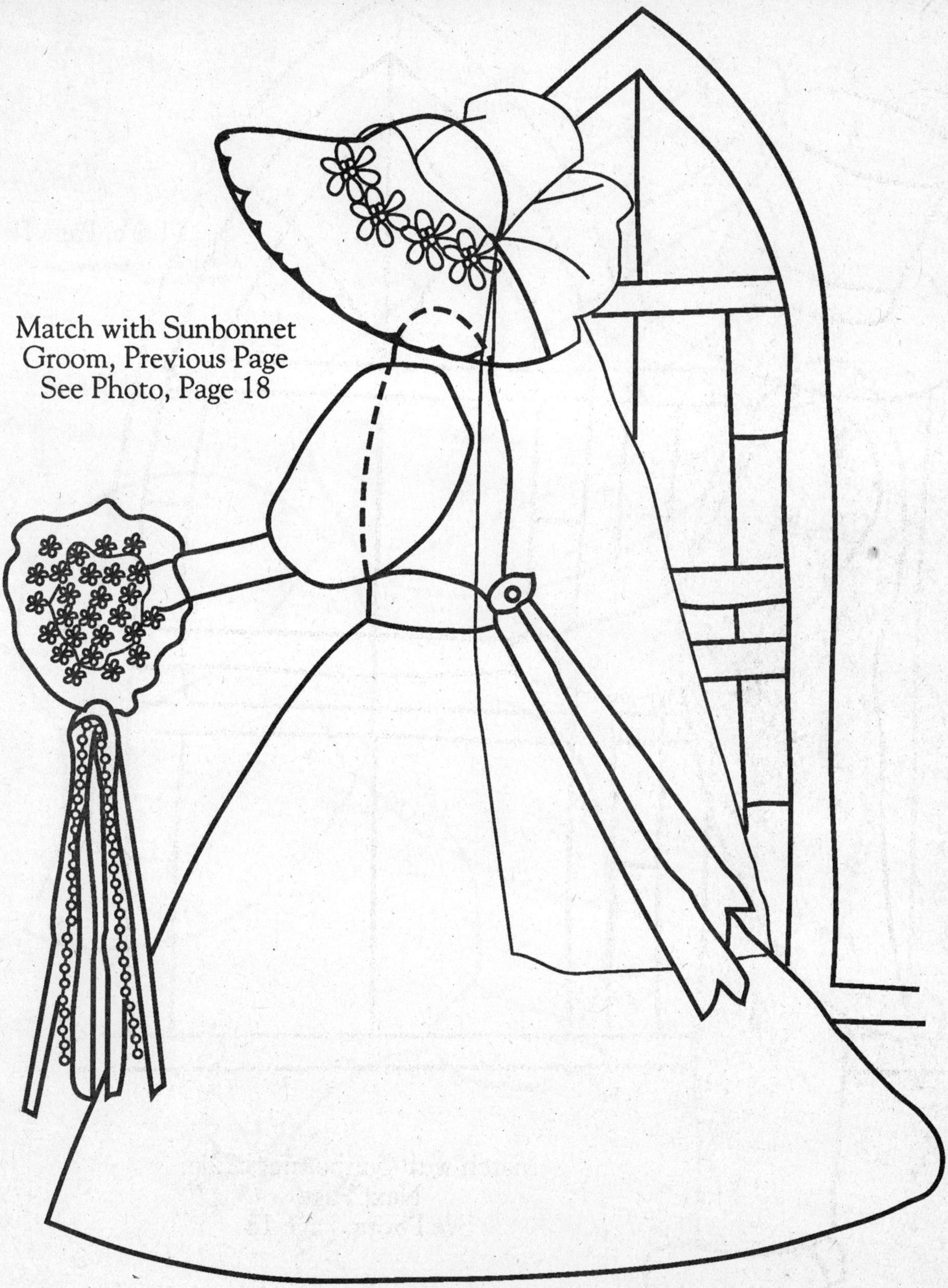

Sunbonnet FAMILY REUNION

Fairy Godmother
Ruth Reinmund • Ottumwa, IA

See Photo, Page 18

Adapted from a *Quilter's Newsletter Magazine* pattern

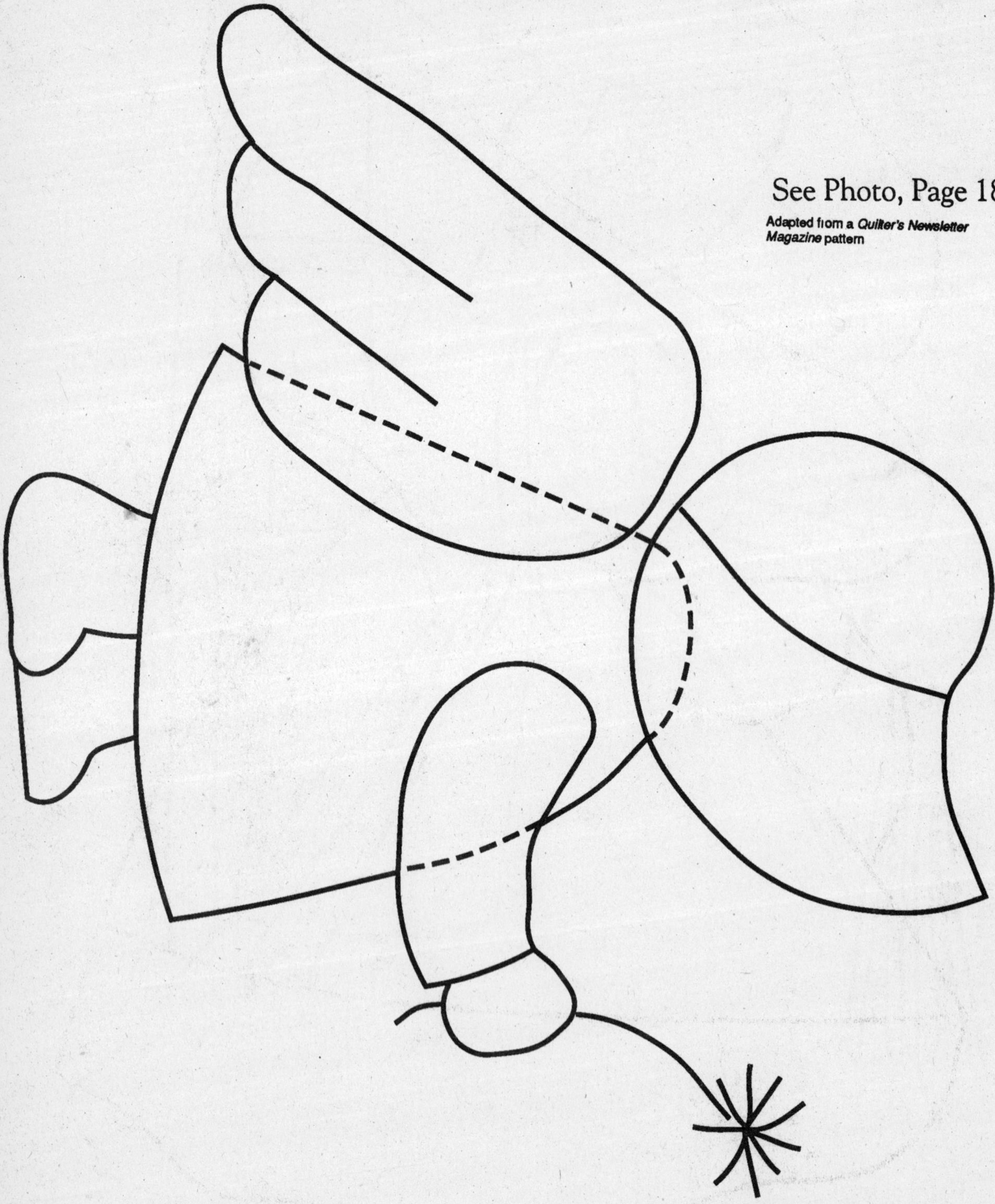

Sunbonnet Baby
Pearl Dawson • Patterson, VA

See Photo, Page 18

Angel Sue
Joyce Stewart • Rexburg, ID

See Photo, Page 18

Sunday Morning
Annis Davis • Darlington, PA

Adapted from *Stitch 'N Sew Quilt's* Calendar
Quilt © Edie Haynie

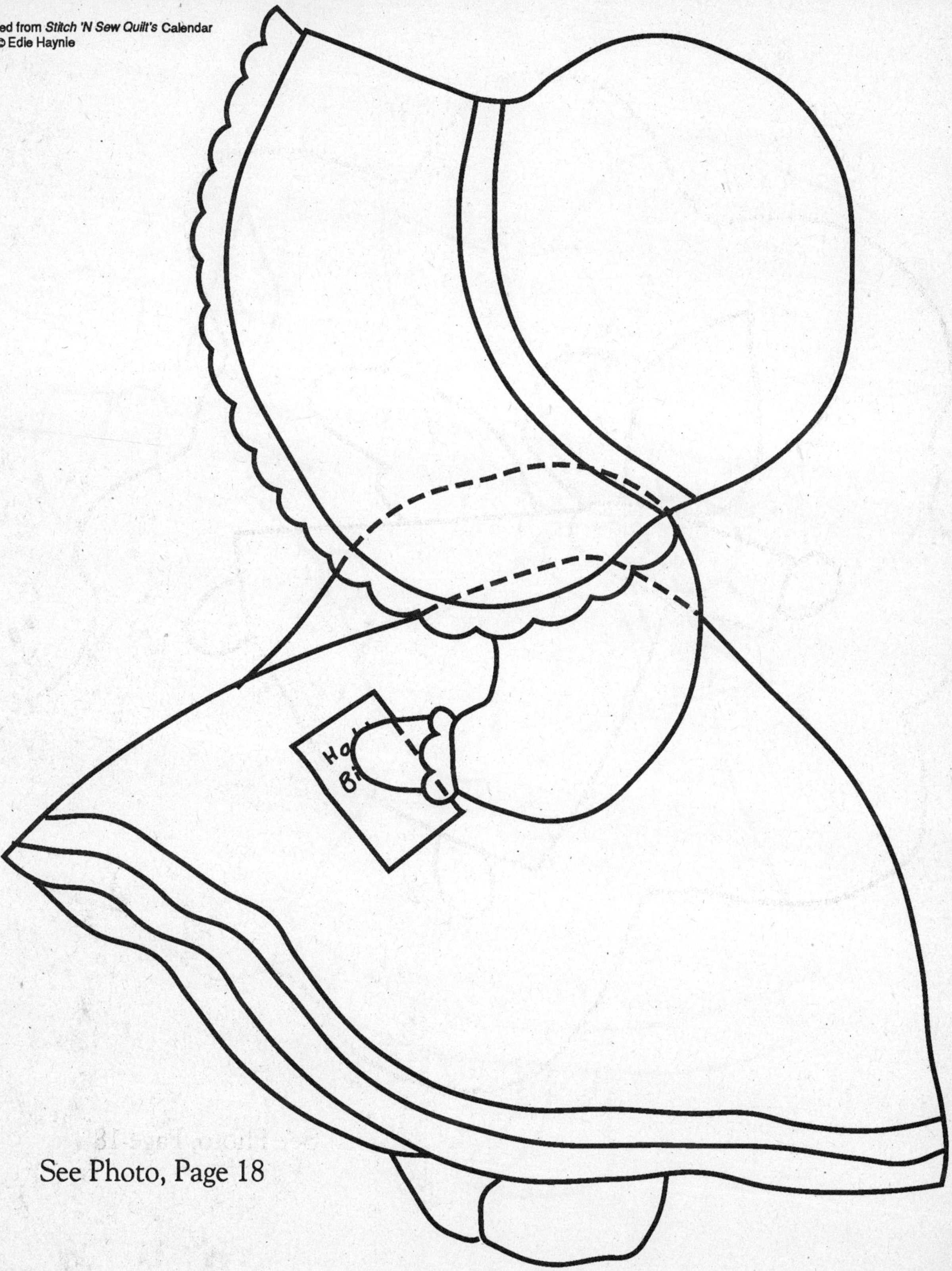

See Photo, Page 18

Sunbonnet FAMILY REUNION

Springtime Anne
Robin Koenig • Butterfield, MO

See Photo, Page 19

Carrying Firewood
Thelma Wendel Kerkman • Lawrence, KS

See Photo, Page 19

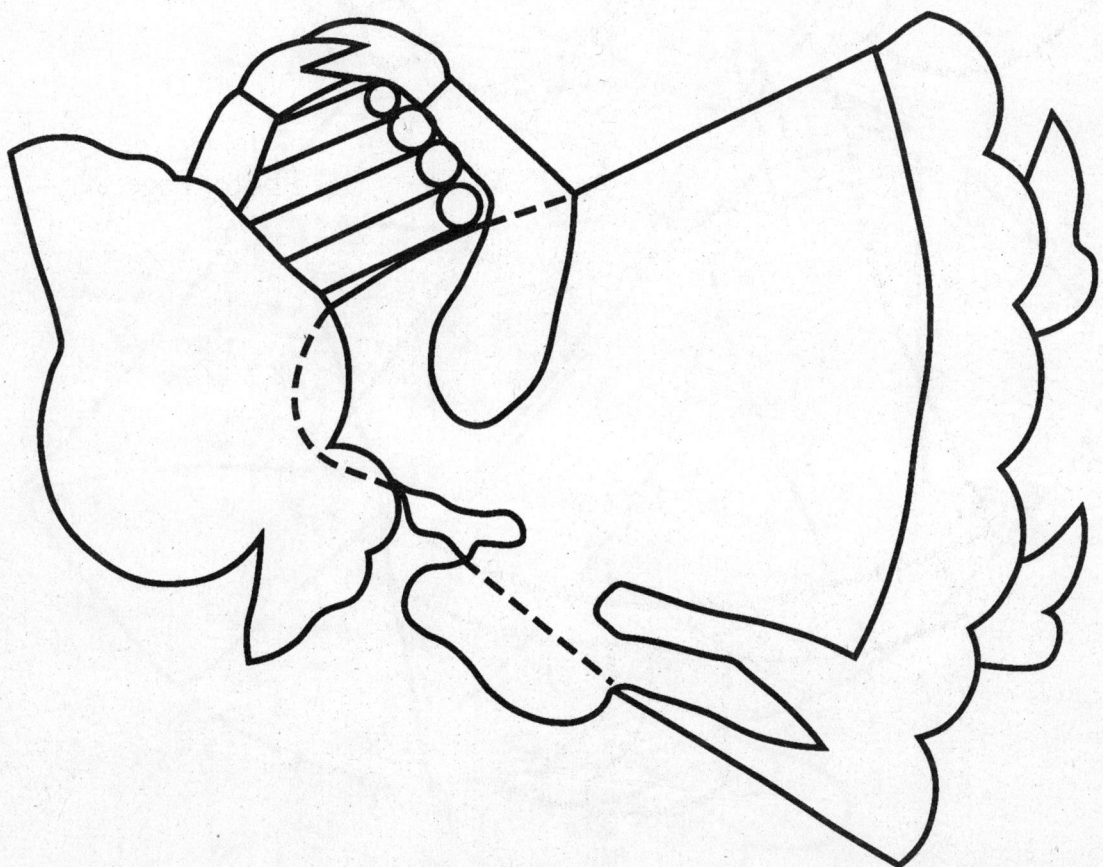

Shepherd Sue
Wanda Peternel • Phoenix, AZ

See Photo, Page 19

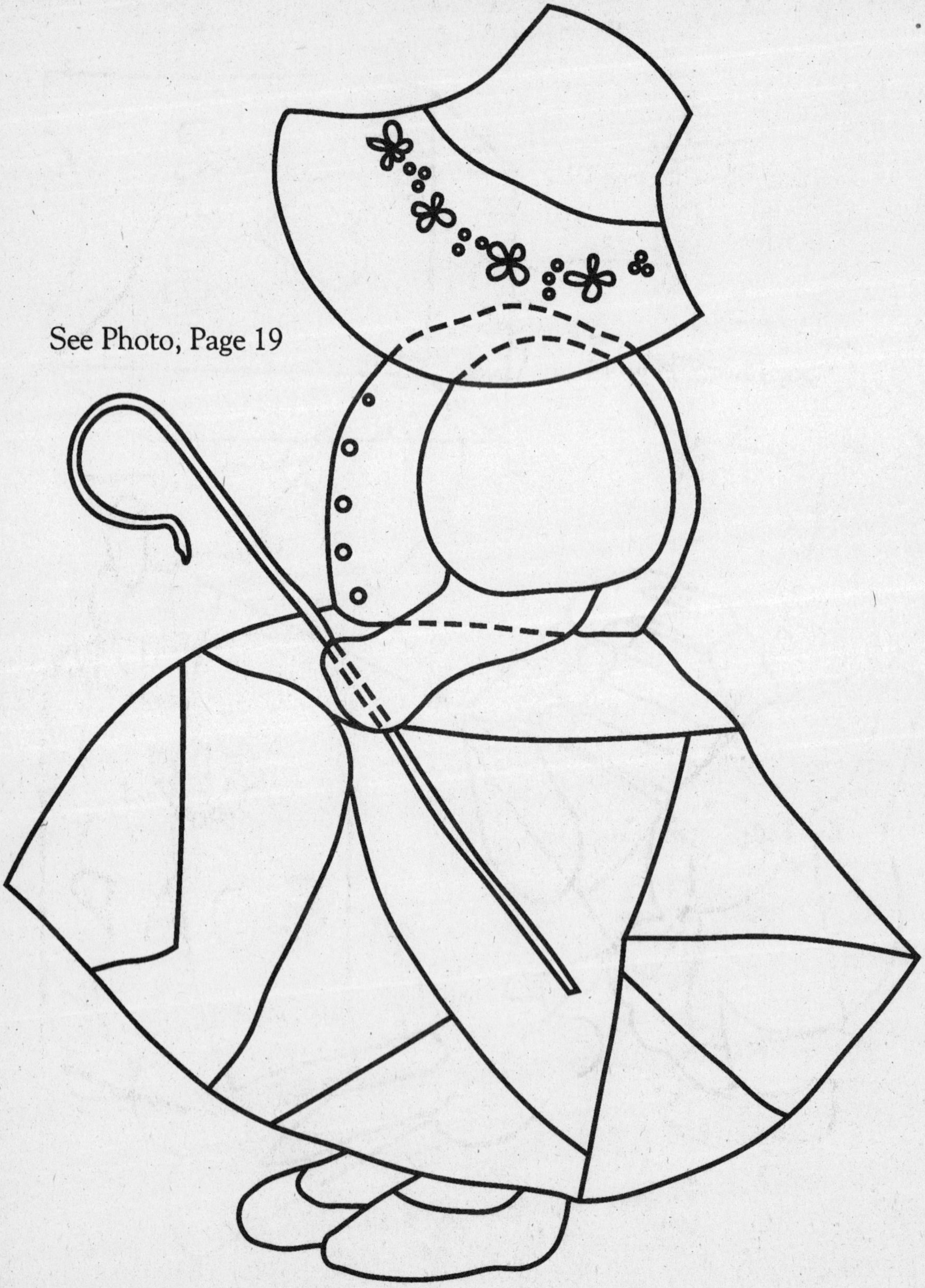

Making Soap
Thelma Wendel Kerkman • Lawrence, KS

See Photo, Page 19

Wee Ones
Marie M. Kelly • Hemet, CA

See Photo, Page 19

Sue's Easter Eggs
Nancy Scoville-Sartor • Moberly, MO

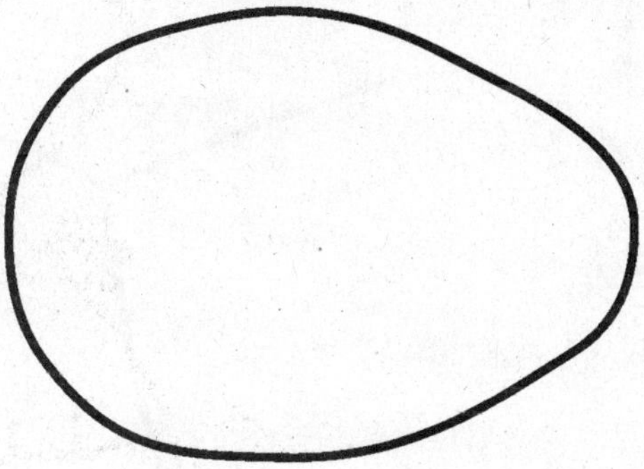

Cut 12 Eggs
See Photo, Page 19

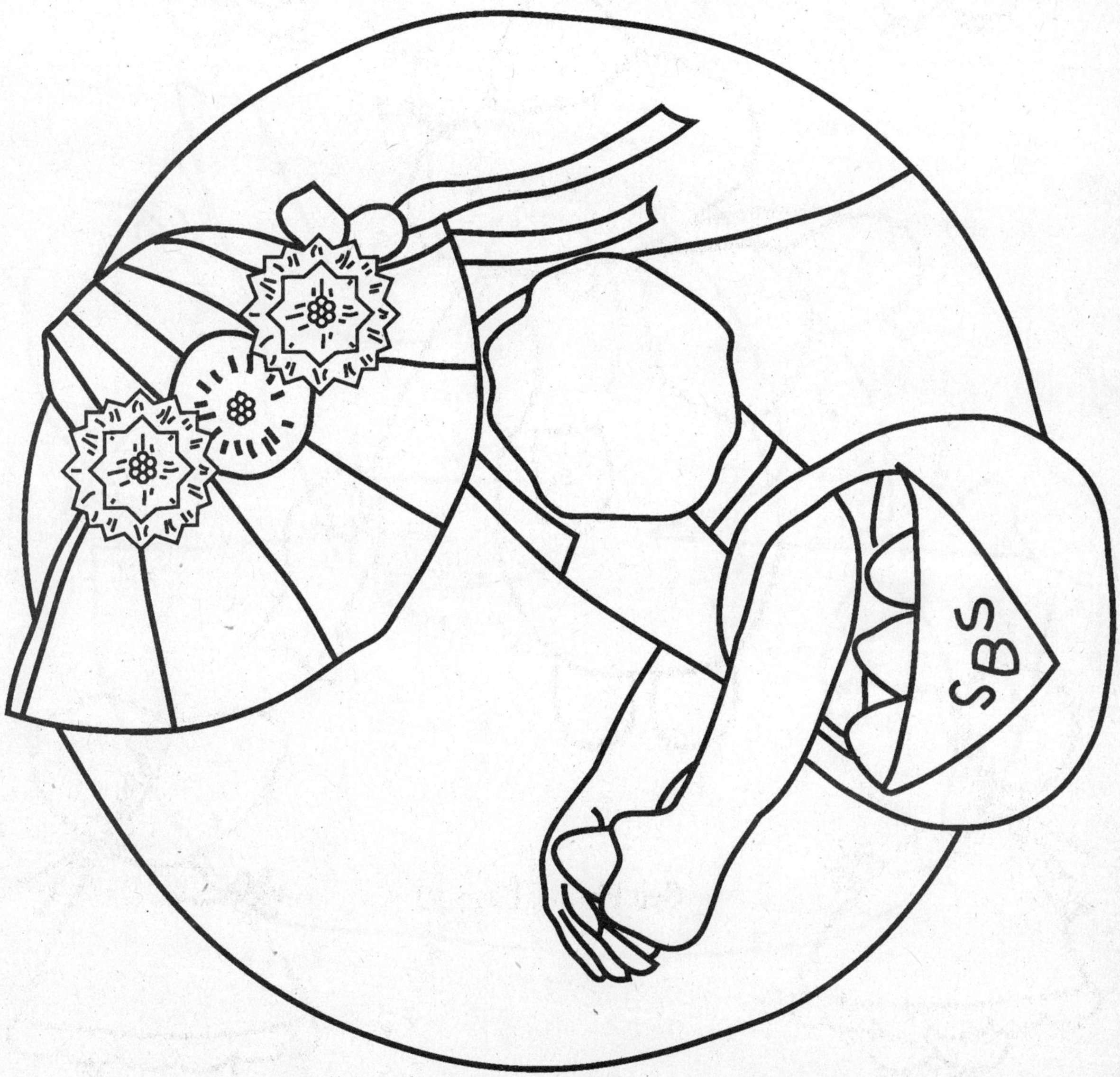

Sunbonnet Sue, The Fisherwoman
Dethel Snow • Vancouver, B.C., Canada

See Photo, Page 19

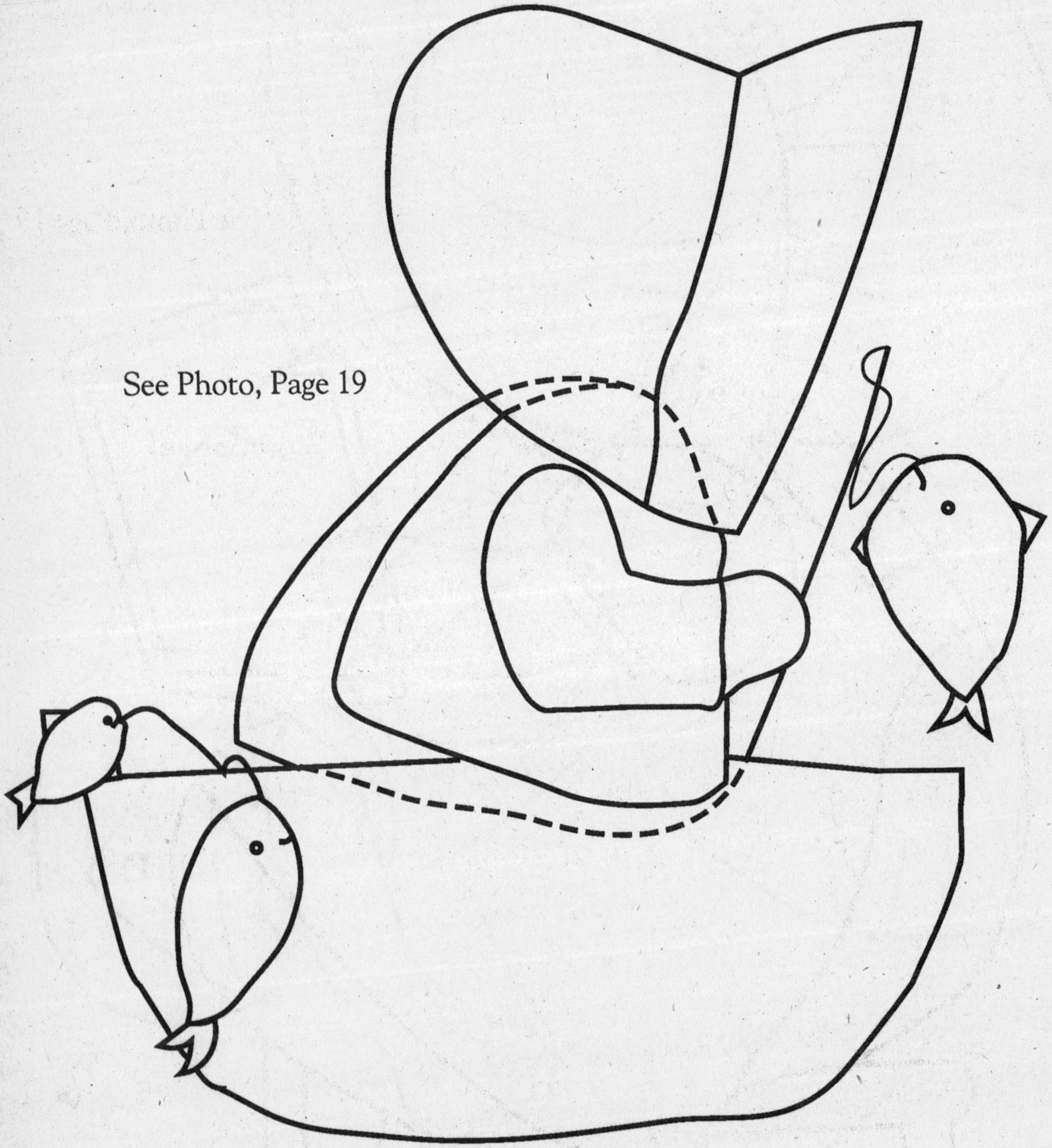

Joy Of Reading
Norma Amamoto • Bethel Park, PA

See Photo, Page 19

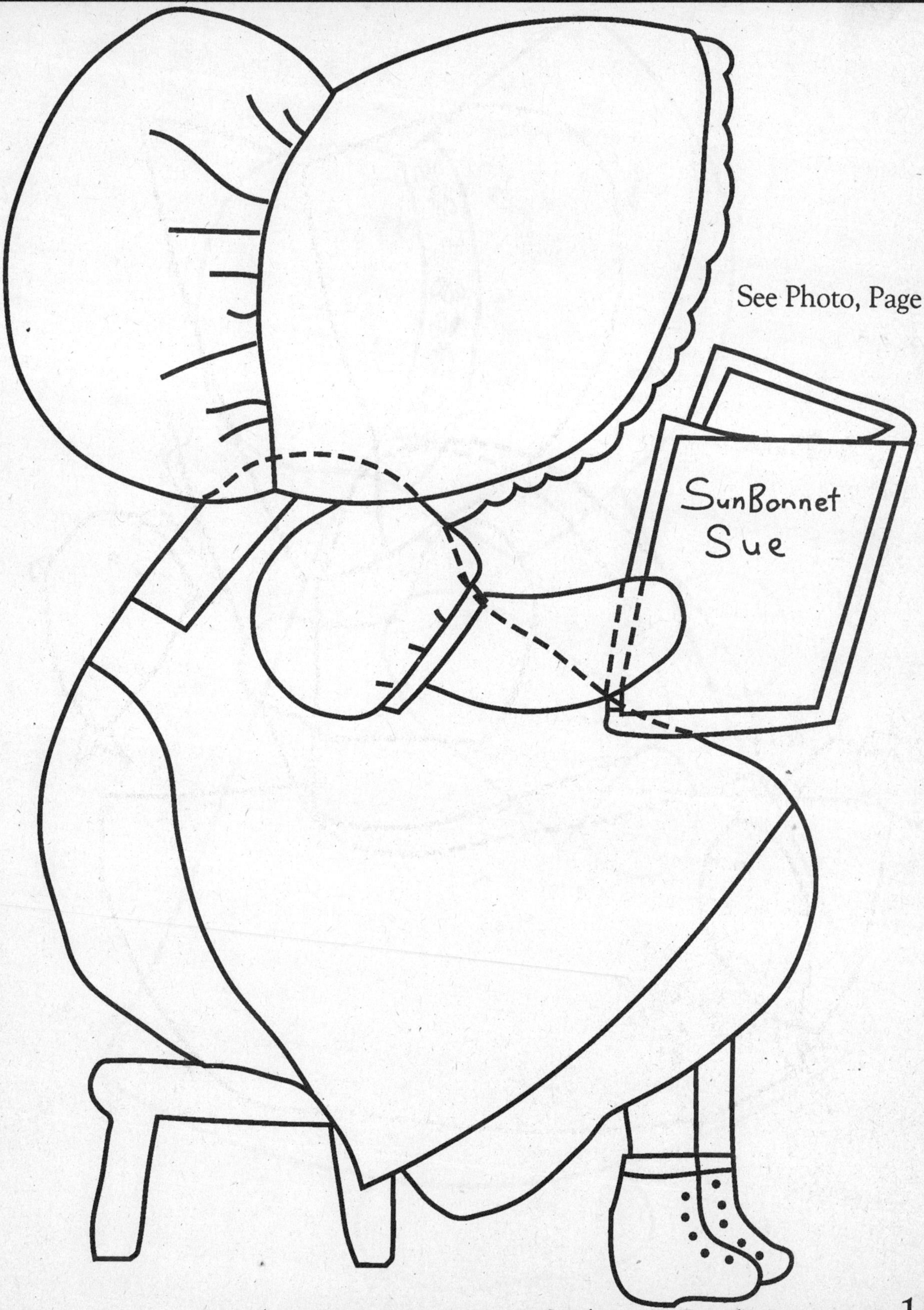

Sunbonnet Sue
Barbara White • Kingwood, WV

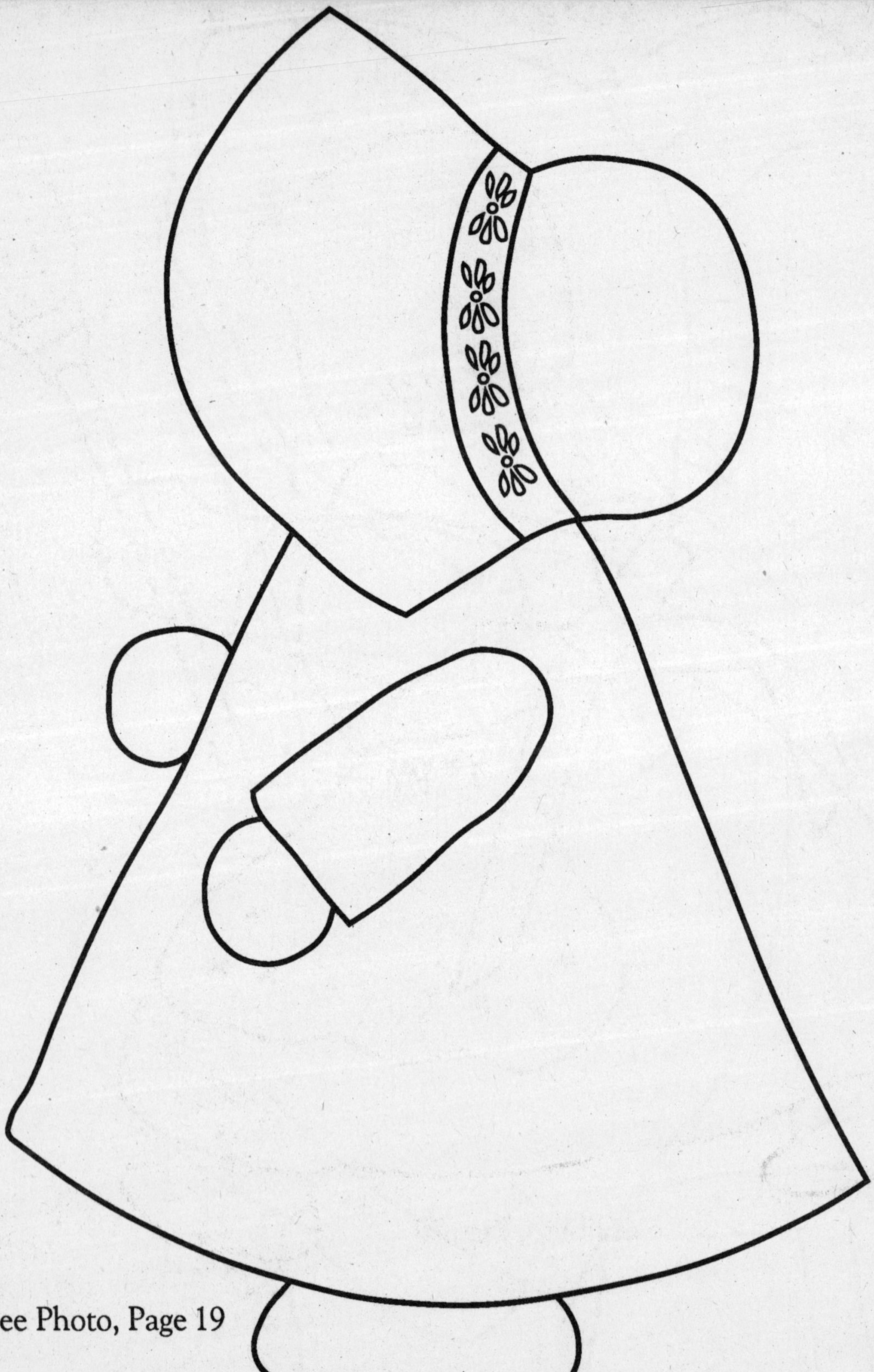

See Photo, Page 19

Go Get Them, Lady Dutch
Alta Rymer • Clovis, CA

See Photo, Page 20

Sunbonnet FAMILY REUNION

Treasure
Louise Butler • Sacramento, CA

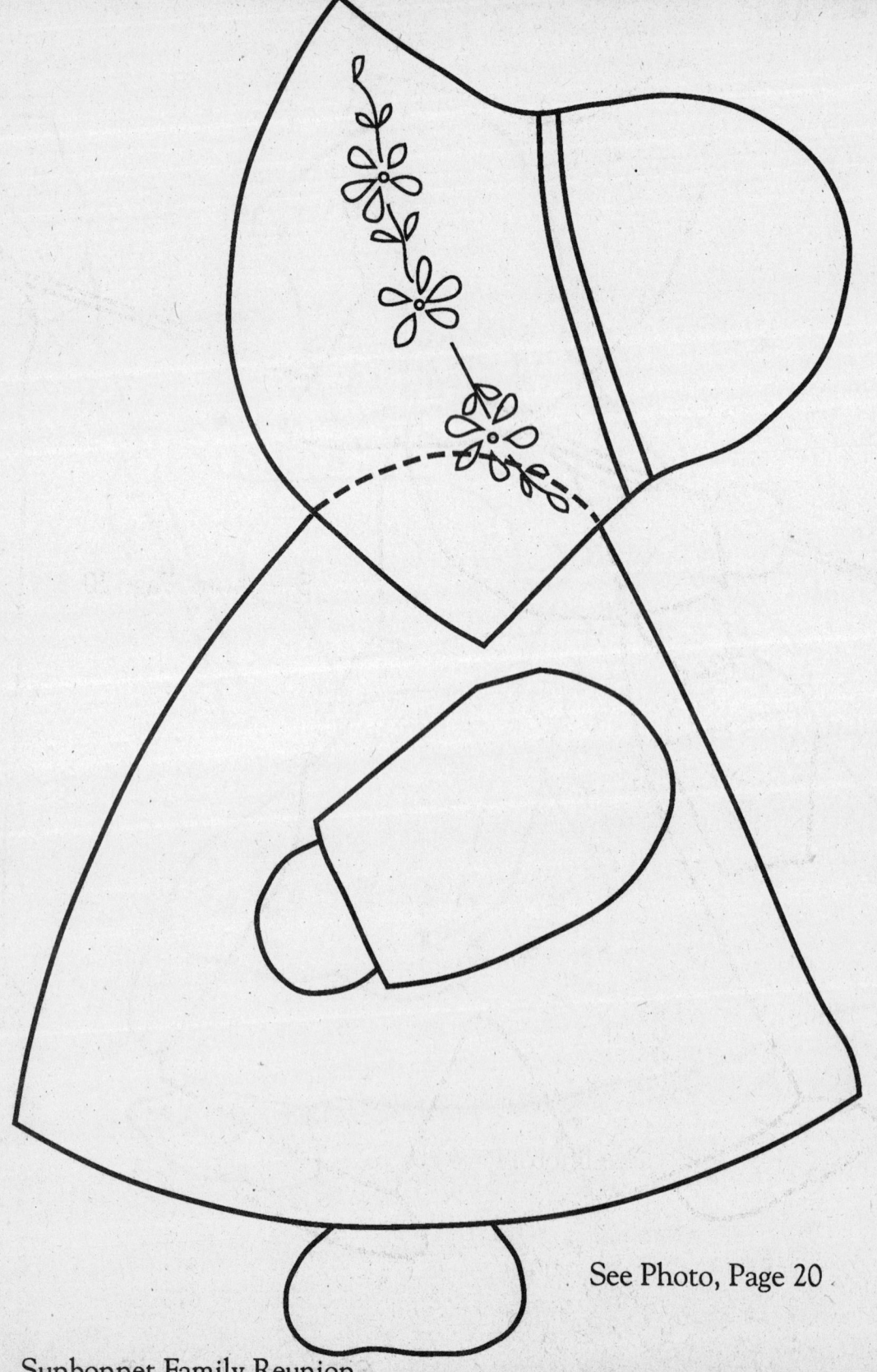

See Photo, Page 20

Fishing Sam
Kelly Groves • Houston, TX

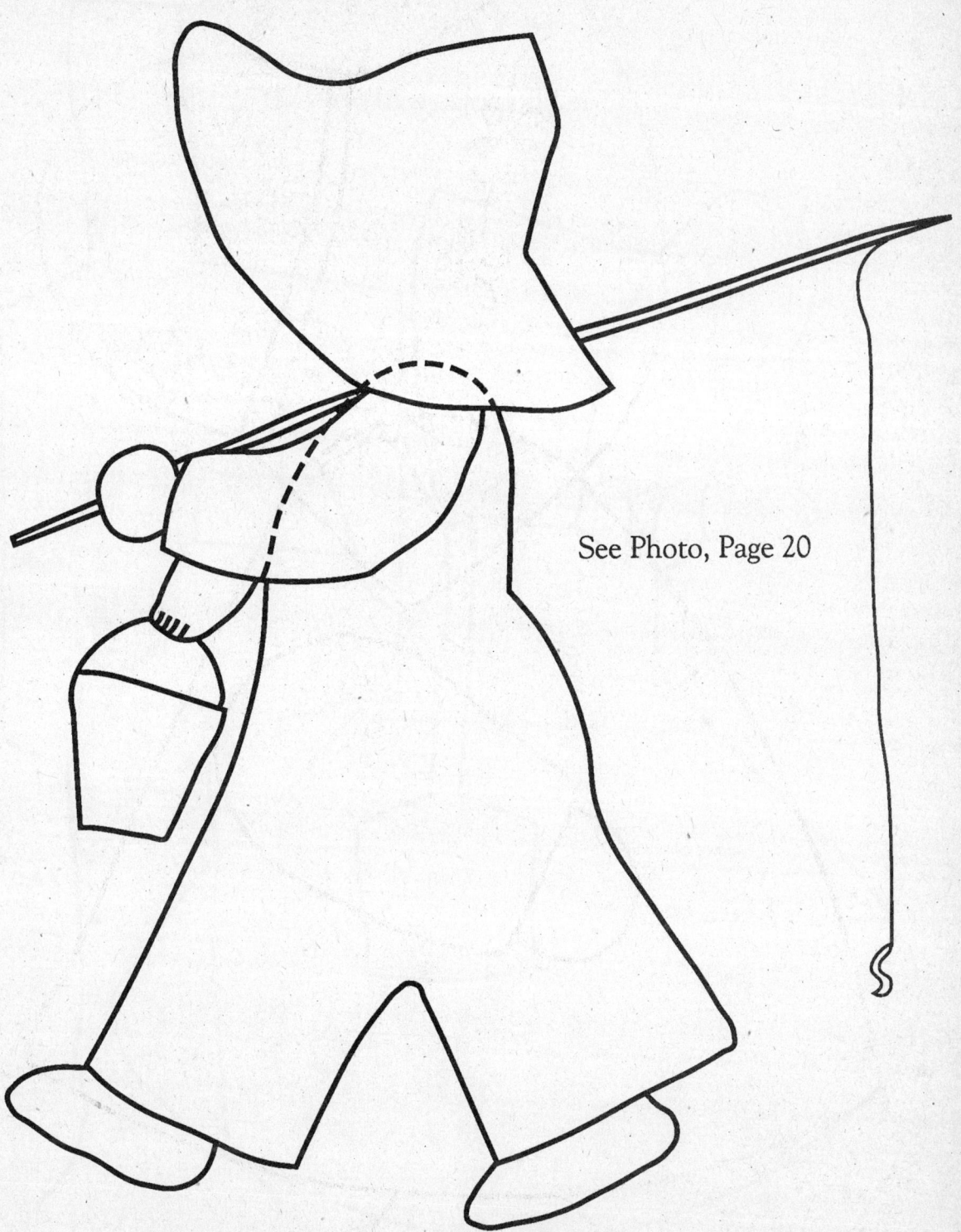

See Photo, Page 20

Sunbonnet Family Reunion 153

Sunbonnet FAMILY REUNION

In The Mail
Pauline Loeffler • Inman, KS

See Photo, Page 20

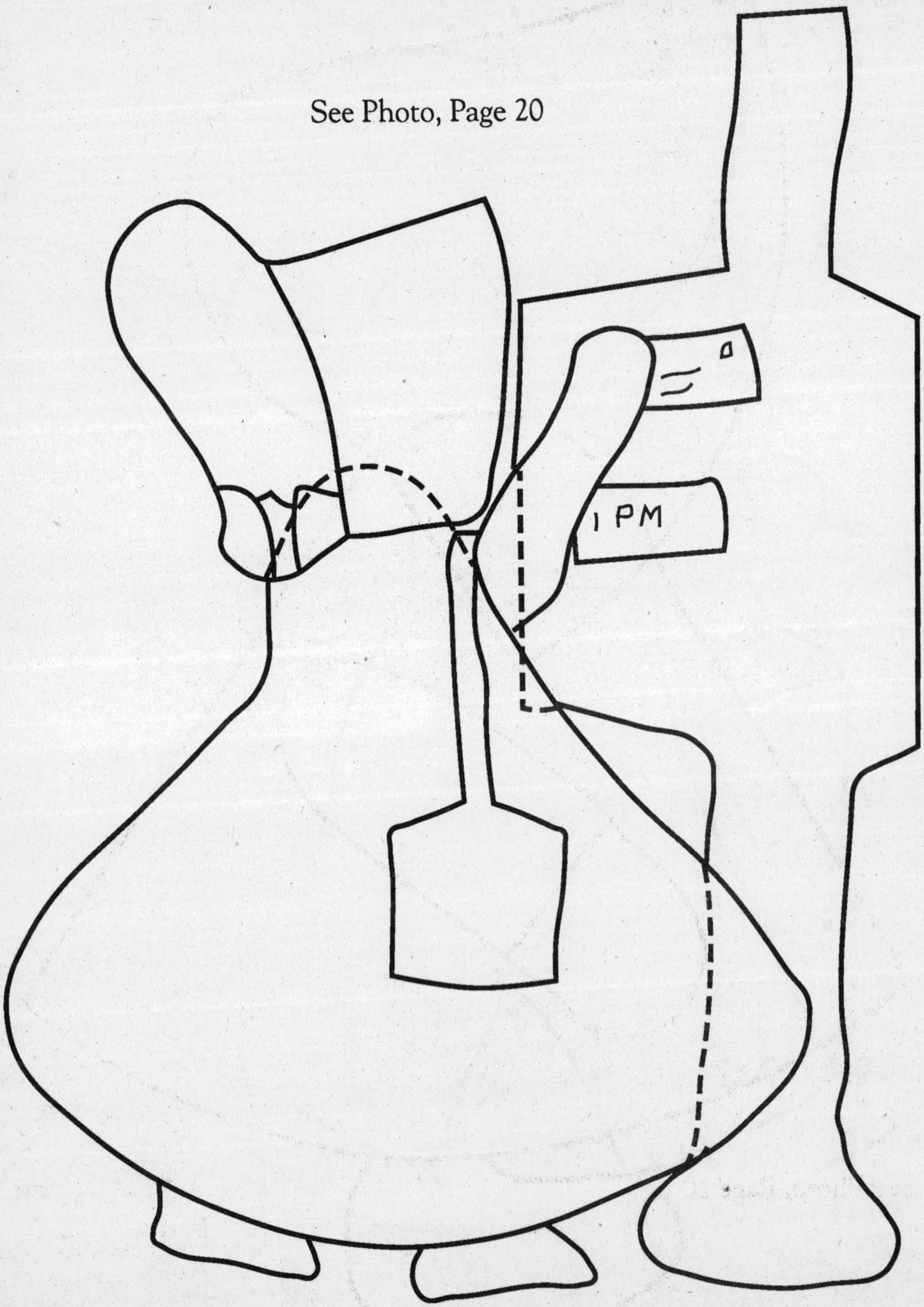

1930s Sunbonnet Girl
Dorothy M. Schomburg • Arlington Heights, IL

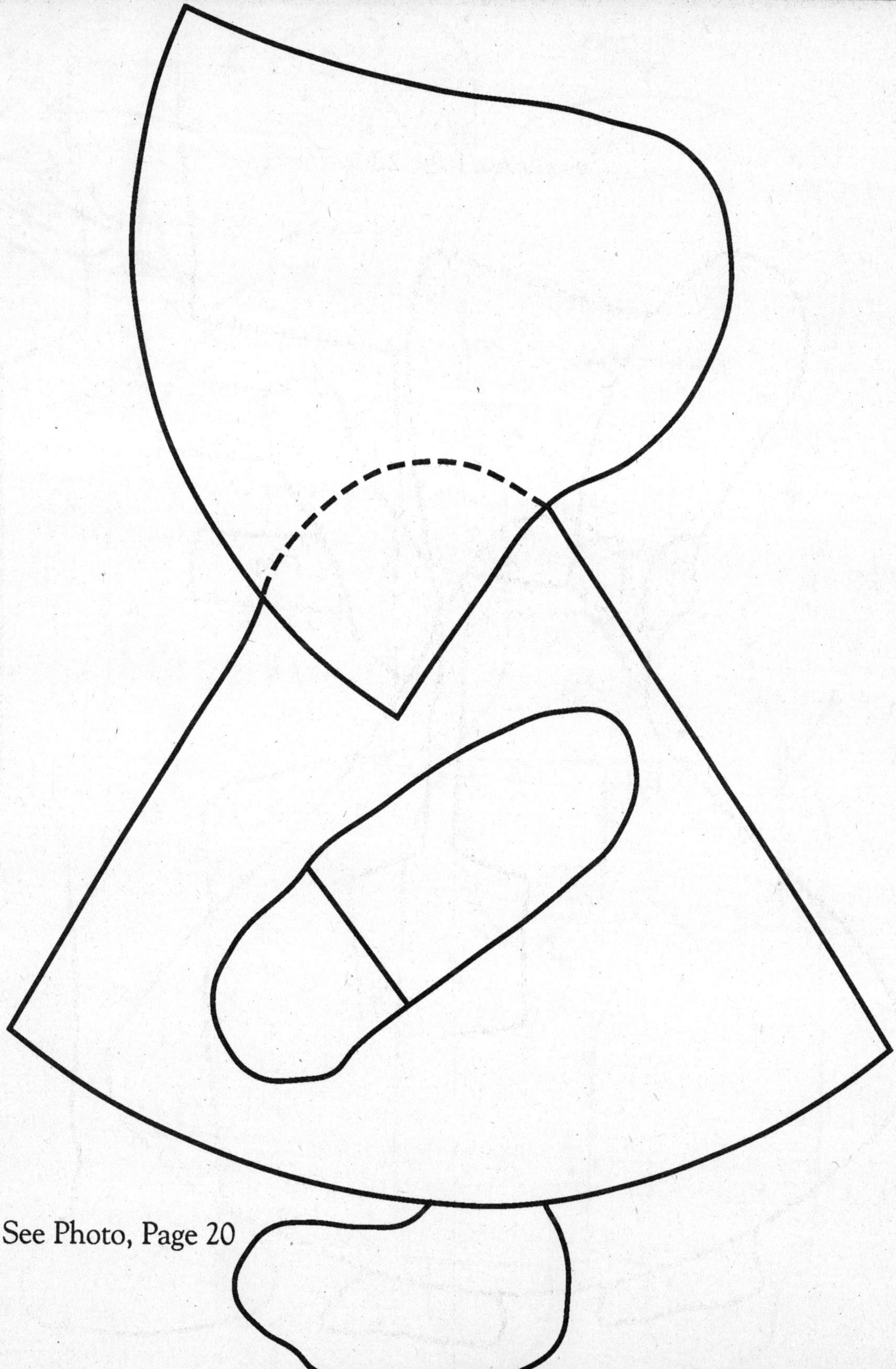

See Photo, Page 20

Sam & Squirrel
Pauline Loeffler • Inman, KS

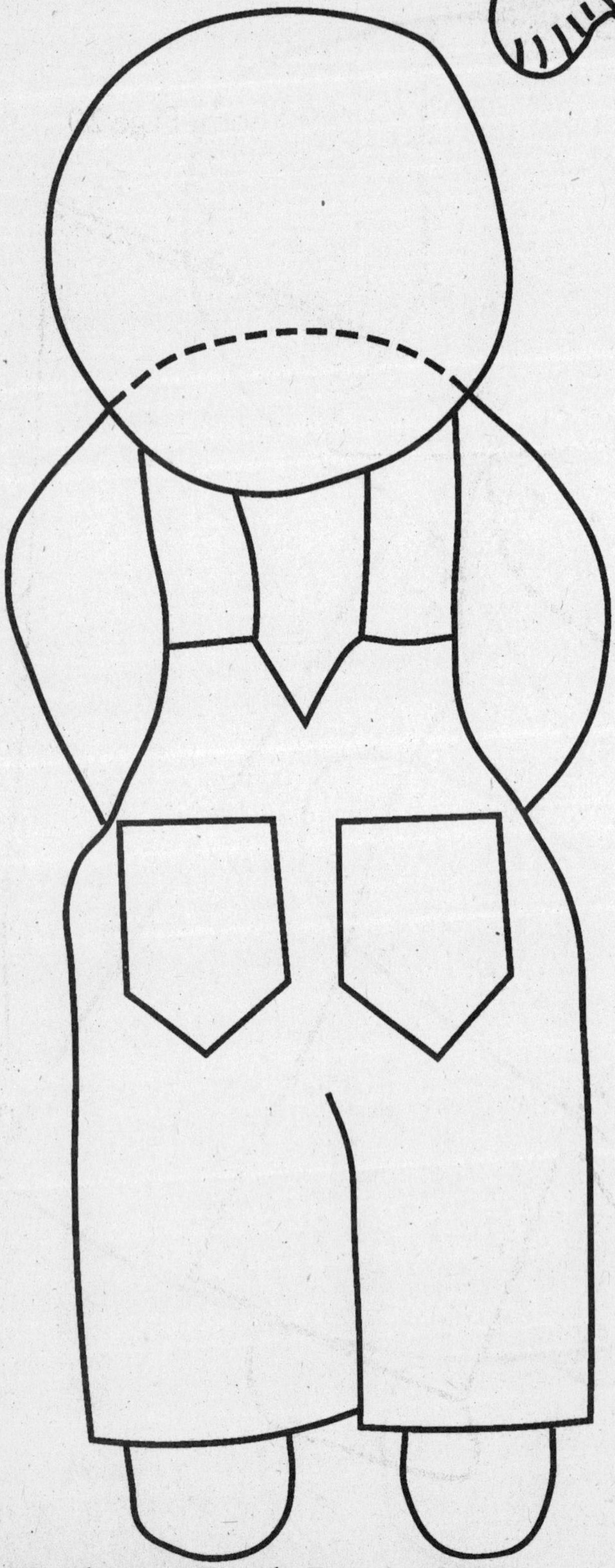

See Photo, Page 20

1940s Sam
Mylinda Marie Groves • Lubbock, TX

 Sunbonnet FAMILY REUNION

See Photo, Page 20

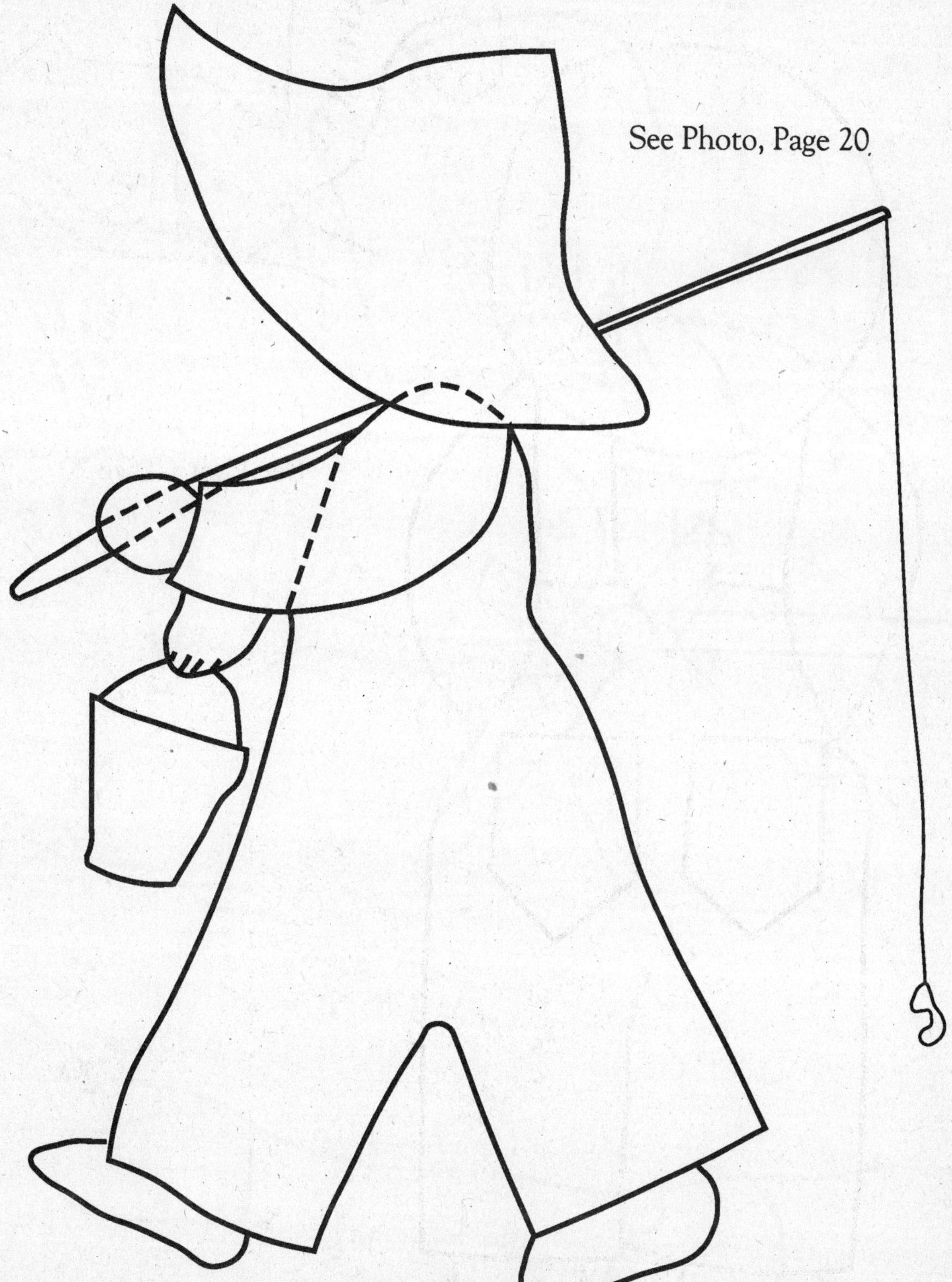

Sunbonnet FAMILY REUNION

Mad At Dirt
Alta Rymer • Clovis, CA

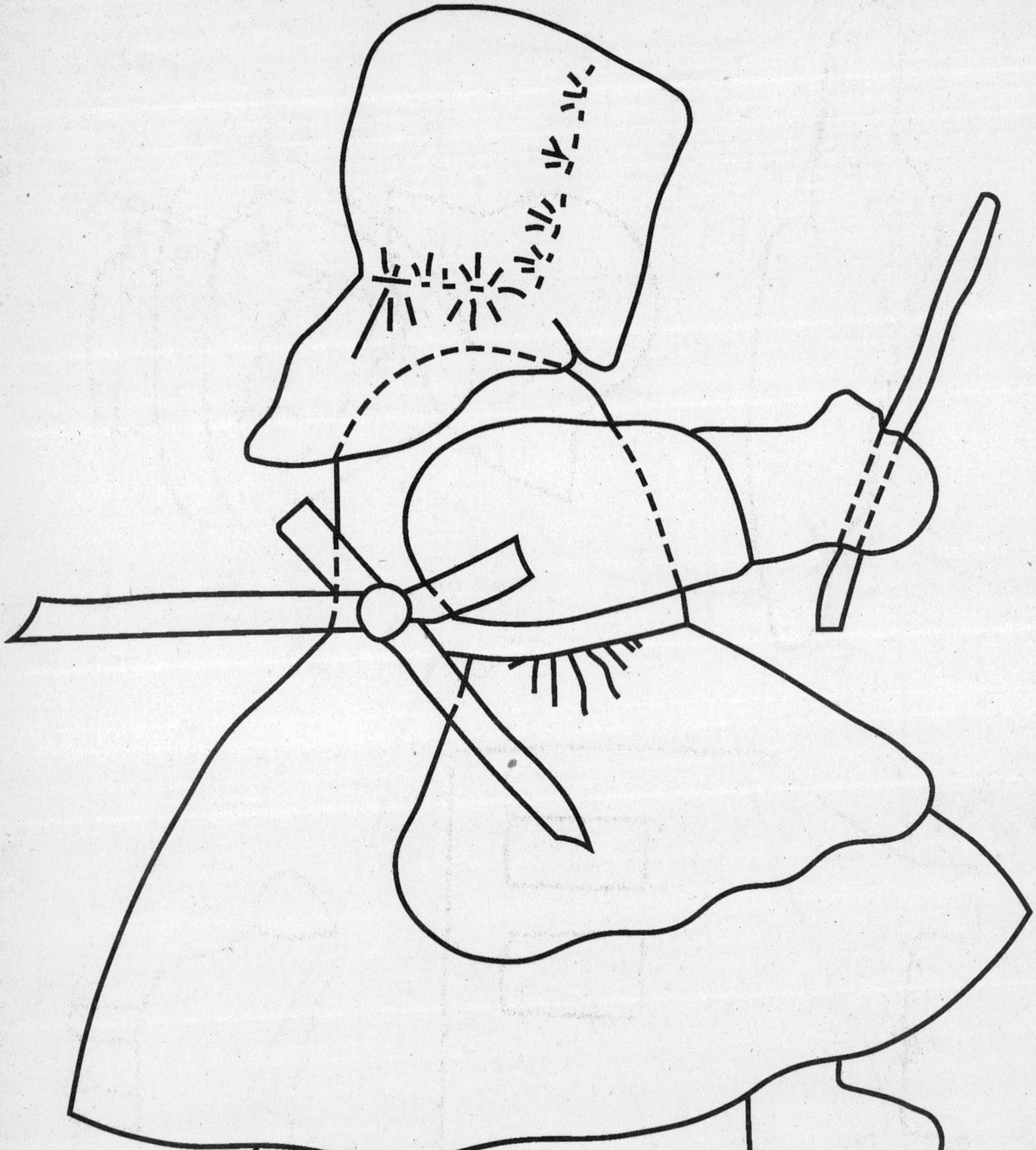

See Photo, Page 20

Sunbonnet Little Lambs
Jennifer James Grupe • Liverpool, TX

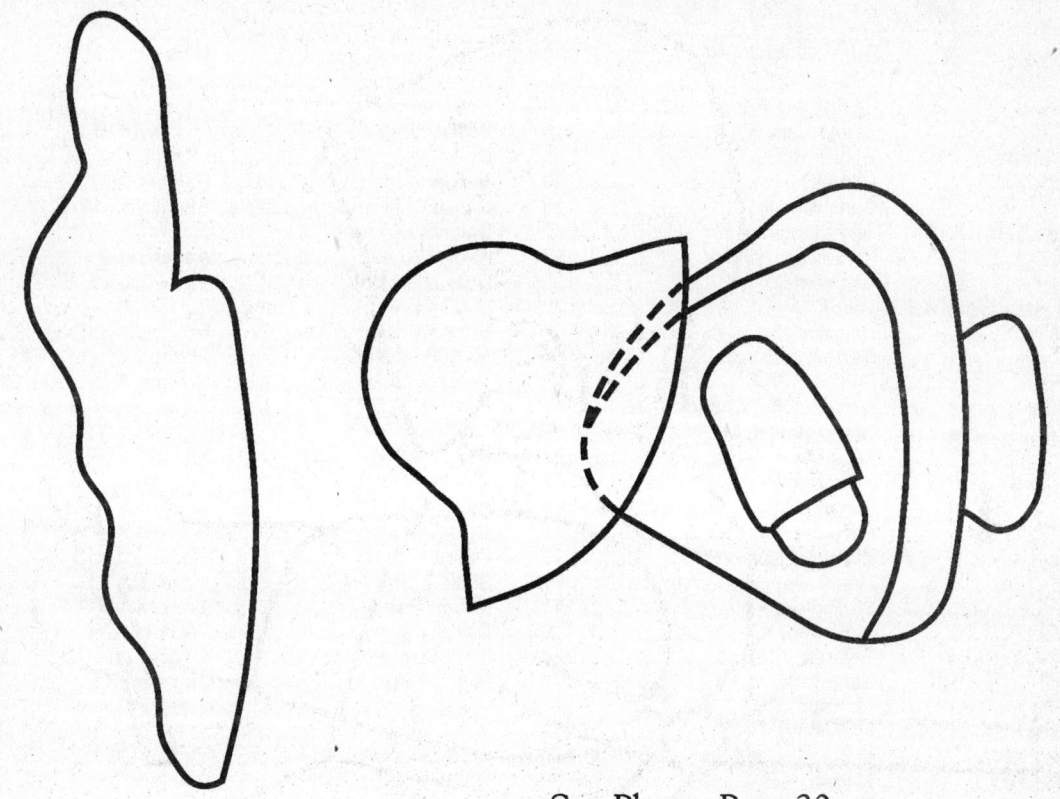

See Photo, Page 20

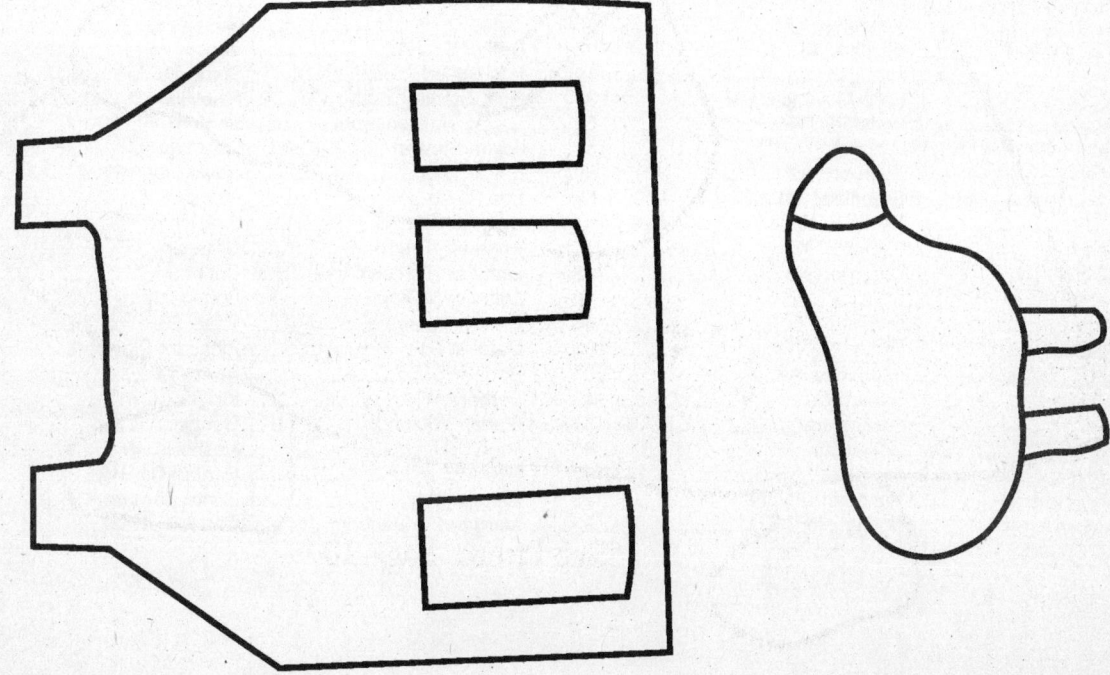

Index

Name	Location	Page
Norma I. Abbott	Gardner, KS	108
Barbara Alexcites	Lenexa, KS	56
Philis R. Alongi	Anaheim, CA	35
Norma Amamoto	Bethel Park, PA	149
Sandra A. Anderson	Lincoln, NE	32,85
Sandra Andrews	Medina, OH	70
Eleanor Bain	Carlinville, IL	115
Linda Baker	San Clemente, CA	36,37
Louise Barney	Broadview Heights, OH	97
Ruth Barr	Chesterfield, MO	90
Mary Lu Beemer-Schofield	Lenox, IA	135
Margaret Bender	Danville, CA	107
Debby Bingham	Baytown, TX	112
Rita J. Blake	Baldwin, PA	111
Ginette Bourque	Kanata, Ont., Canada	40,41
Betty Boyink	Grand Haven, MI	62
Claudia Brownfield	Aspermont, TX	69
Louise Butler	Sacramento, CA	152
Maryanne Cammarata	Summit, AR	99
Sandra L. Christiansen	Phoenix, AZ	45,46
Wilma Crawford	Brainerd, MN	120
Linda Elaine Crowell	Greenville, OH	72
Annis Davis	Darlington, PA	141
Pearl Dawson	Patterson, VA	139
Sandra Dick	Roswell, NM	84
Ida Mae Drommer	Norton, KS	78
Geneva Dunster	Atchison, KS	65
Marge Eakins	La Puente, CA	25,122
Susan Jean Faber	Dyer, IN	136,137
Mildred Fauquet	Lincoln, NE	30
Maryon Peterson Ferguson	Eugene, OR	86
Theresa Filley	Leavenworth, KS	98
Nurlie Foster	Haynesville, LA	31
Mary Ellen Frenzel	Oshkosh, WI	103
Carrie Mae Gehrke	Libby, MT	53
Mickey K. Geismar	Gonzales, LA	66
Gertrude M. Gerkey	Decatur, MI	102
Mary Gish	Michigan City, IN	119
Evelyn A. Gorek	North Royalton, OH	34
Kelly Groves	Houston, TX	153
Mylinda Marie Groves	Lubbock, TX	157
Jennifer James Grupe	Liverpool, TX	159
Mary Jo Gussert	Greenleaf, WI	59
Colleen Hall	Overland Park, KS	117
Oma Dee Heard	Dimmitt, TX	54
Sandra J. Heid	Cherokee, IA	83
Ann S. Huffman	Choctaw, OK	109
Nell Humphrey	Dimmitt, TX	55
Ann Jensen	Richland, WA	106
Catherine R. Jones	Fairbanks, AK	121
Marie M. Kelly	Hemet, CA	146
Lavona Keltner	Camdenton, MO	68,118
Irma K. Kendall	Hollandale, MS	60
Thelma Wendel Kerkman	Lawrence, KS	143,145
Mildred Kitchens	Kennean City, FL	123
Janelle Jones Knox	Springfield, MO	39
Robin Koenig	Butterfield, MO	142
Norma N. Locke	Gaston, OR	26,27
Pauline Loeffler	Inman, KS	44,154,156
Phyllis Long	Lindsey, OH	134
Doris Lust	Dimmit, TX	51,52
Margaret Manti	Parma, OH	91
Susan L. McMullin	Sunnyside, WA	76
Dolores M. Merle	Elmwood Park, IL	87
Kate Mitchell	Anderson, IN	126
Dixie D. Moody	Yale, OK	64
Sue Moore	Tulsa, OK	75
Mary Ann Morris Newlon	St. Petersburg, FL	89
Mary B. Mulligan	Abbotsford, B.C., Canada	81,82
Tammie Nisbilt	Dimmit, TX	48
Setsako T. O'Neill	Wyoming, MI	61
Vicki Olson	Wyoming, MN	124
Kati Olson	Wyoming, MN	28
Wanda Peternel	Phoenix, AZ	144
Pauline Petty	Nashville, TN	128
Elizabeth J. Prather	Grapevine, TX	43
Leona E. Price	Florissant, MO	29,88
Betty L. Purkey	Irvine, CA	129
Miriam Reed	Grandview, MO	100
Dorothy Reif	Windsor, Ont., Canada	110
Ruth Reinmund	Ottumwa, IA	138
Mrs. George A. Richard	Emporia, KS	77
Felicia Ryan	Newport News, VA	47,49
Alta Rymer	Clovis, CA	73,151,158
Shari Schmidt	Turpin, OK	131
Dorothy M. Schomburg	Arlington Heights, IL	155
Nancy Scoville-Sartor	Moberly, MO	147
Mary Self	Gallion, AL	130
Ann Sgro	Crystal River, FL	92,93
Helen Siegel	New Port Richey, FL	57,58
Irene Sliwinski	Keene, NH	71
Janet Smith	Gonzales, TX	105
Dethel Snow	Vancouver, B.C., Canada	148
Lou Speed	Starkville, MS	95
Ruth Starkey	Pineville, LA	63
Louise H. Stenstrom	Sanford, FL	125,127
Joyce Stewart	Rexburg, ID	140
Esther Stone	Davis City, IA	104
Lee Streib	Pleasant Hill, CA	74
Judy M. Sweets	Lawrence, KS	94
Annadell Teems	Granbury, TX	67,133
Linda M. Throckmorton	Cutler, ME	33
Lois Grace Voigt	Bonner Springs, KS	132
Esther Weisser	Tripp, SD	42
Carol Welch	Pleasant Plains, IL	116
Bonnie White	Boyd, TX	96
Barbara White	Kingwood, WV	150
Mariah Wilson	Gonzales, TX	114
June Wolpert	Nashville, IN	79,80,113
Marian S. Woods	Central City, IA	50
Eleanor Wright	Santa Barbara, CA	38
Margaret Youngberg	Chanute, KS	101